There is a question of equilibri᷉ ▯▯▯▯▯▯ ▯▯▯▯▯▯ as in the physical universe. It ▯▯▯▯▯▯▯ ▯▯▯▯▯▯ Christ, who reestablished this balance on the highest level, after sin had unleashed ruin upon mankind. But some souls are called *to fill up those things that are wanting of the sufferings of Christ in their flesh for His Body*, as Saint Paul tells us. How can this be? Let the story of Sister Maria Bernadette, who was surely one of those souls, lift a corner of the veil and draw you into the mystery. Maybe you too have a part to play.

— **ABBOT PHILIP ANDERSON OSB**, Our Lady of Clear Creek Abbey, Hulbert, Oklahoma

An amazing book! I am grateful to know about Sister Bernadette and the way she gave her life for the conversion of apostate priests. Her vocation as a Benedictine Nun of Perpetual Adoration led her to imitate Jesus' own acceptance of salvific suffering. Because she followed His way, suffering became the most fruitful and joyful path to her life's fulfillment. Her story will help you turn your own difficulties — whether large or small — into the currency of pure love.

— **MOTHER IMMACULATA FRANKEN OSBAP**, Prioress, Bene-dictines of Perpetual Adoration, Tegelen, The Netherlands

Sister Bernadette was one of those souls who, while living with the Church, the liturgy, and the Scriptures, allow themselves to be led by the Spirit to pray and to suffer — generously and cheerfully. She made an offering of her life, and in these pages we can learn to do the same. This book is a roadmap to true happiness, not only in the afterlife, but beginning here and now.

— **SCOTT HAHN**, author of *The Lamb's Supper: The Mass as Heaven on Earth*

The life of Sister Bernadette of the Cross is vividly detailed here. Her role as a child of God, in a world ravaged and abused by war and corruption, comes across as both heroic and ordinary. As we go through the pages, her very soul seems to be honed and polished before our eyes; she is both reduced and glorified by her pains. Her story is an illustration of what it means to suffer in Christ, and for the sins of others, and is given great immediacy and vitality by the examples of her beautiful art. Her words are meat for those who wonder about the role of suffering in life.

— **SALLY READ**, author of *Night's Bright Darkness*

FOR THEIR SAKE
I CONSECRATE MYSELF

For Their Sake I Consecrate Myself

SISTER
MARIA BERNADETTE
OF THE CROSS
(RÓŻA MARIA WOLSKA)
Benedictine Nun of Perpetual Adoration
1927–1963

JADWIGA STABIŃSKA, OSBap

Translated by
Justyna Krukowska

Originally published as *Za Nich Poświęcam Siebie* by Wydawnictwo
Sióstr Loretanek
(ul. Żeligowskiego 16/20, 04-476 Warszawa),
© Siostry Sakramentki, Warszawa 2008

English edition © Arouca Press 2022
Translation © Silverstream Priory 2022

ISBN: 978-1-990685-04-0 (pbk)
ISBN: 978-1-990685-05-7 (hardcover)

Arouca Press
PO Box 55003
Bridgeport PO
Waterloo, ON N2J 3G0
Canada
www.aroucapress.com
Send inquiries to info@aroucapress.com

CONTENTS

AUTHOR'S NOTE
TO THE POLISH EDITION

IN HER LETTERS, SISTER BERNADETTE QUOTES SCRIP-
ture mostly from memory. No stylistic corrections of her writings
were made, and original punctuation and capitalization were preserved.
The names of those living persons who gave their consent have been
included. In other cases, only the first letters of the first and last name,
or first or last name only are given. The book's title, *For Their Sake I
Consecrate Myself*, echoes Christ's words from the Gospel according
to Saint John, *pro eis ego sanctifico meipsum* (Jn 17:19).

A NOTE ON THIS EDITION

THIS TRANSLATION REPRESENTS A SLIGHT REVISION of the original book; it departs from the Polish original in a few places where it was thought opportune for clarity or style. These modifications were made with the consent of the Warsaw monastery. Not all the idiosyncrasies present in Sr Bernadette's own writings have been consistently retained in the present edition. Although a few footnotes are adapted from material in the original edition, the majority have been added to this edition by the translator and the monks of Silverstream Priory to elucidate the text's Polish and monastic content for English-speaking readers. The original spelling of most Polish proper names has been preserved.

All biblical quotations have been taken from the Douay-Rheims Bible, which is a translation from the Latin Vulgate, unless otherwise noted. There are occasional discrepancies in verse numbers between the Millennium Bible (the Polish translation used in the Polish text) and the Douay-Rheims Bible. Missal texts have been taken from the *1962 Roman Catholic Daily Missal* (Kansas City, MO: Angelus Press, 2004).

The title of the book has been translated following Christ's words from the Gospel of Saint John, per the author's note. In Polish, the title could have a twofold meaning of *I sanctify myself for them*, or *I sacrifice myself for them*. The English title is taken from the RSV translation of John 17:19 as "consecrate" captures something of this double meaning.

Unless otherwise noted, all the photographs are courtesy of the Benedictine Nuns of Perpetual Adoration in Warsaw. Special thanks must go to the monks of Tyniec for their assistance in obtaining several additional photographs relating to their Abbey, and likewise to the monks of Solesmes for their kind permission to reproduce music from the 1934 *Antiphonale Monasticum*. All rights reserved for images not noted as being sourced from Wikimedia Commons. Some of the Wikimedia images have been cropped.

FOREWORD

GOD CALLS "MEN AND WOMEN WHO, FROM THE BEGIN-
ning of the Church until the end, are touched by God's love and feel
called to follow the Lamb, once sacrificed and now alive, wherever
he goes."[1]

The book *For Their Sake I Consecrate Myself* is the story of a
Polish Benedictine nun, Sister Bernadette of the Cross, who consciously offered her young life in reparation for priestly infidelities.
God accepted that sacrifice. She was 35 years old, in solemn vows
for eight years. Souls burn with God's love in different ways, always
and in every state, but Providence wants some of them to be better
known to the rest of the world.

Maria Róża Wolska was born in 1927 and died in 1963. She came
from a family of landowners. The years of her youth coincided with
World War II. She was very talented and independent, and had a
choleric temperament. She was a graduate of the Academy of Fine
Arts. In 1950, she became an oblate at the Benedictine Abbey in Tyniec.
A year later she joined the cloistered Benedictine Nuns of Perpetual
Adoration of the Blessed Sacrament in Warsaw, whose monastery was
being rebuilt at the time after having been bombed during the war.
The material conditions were lamentable, but the spiritual life of the
monastery flourished. In Poland, the 1950s and 1960s were the most
difficult years of the Communist regime. Sister Bernadette, under
circumstances which by human standards were not at all conducive
to achieving union with God, flared up like a burning coal.

She had a sense of imminent death, God quickly purified and
simplified her, and she surrendered to Him. After news of priestly
infidelities, with the approval of her superiors she offered her life
to God as a sacrifice of reparation for the sins of priests. "Cut me
into strips, but let them return to You and give You glory." She died
following complications from a simple medical procedure.

For Their Sake I Consecrate Myself is a testimony written by a sister
from her community, Jadwiga Stabińska, author of several books,

---

1   John Paul II, *Vita Consecrata* 23.

mostly dealing with monastic and hagiographic themes. With great precision she gathered the accounts of sisters, relatives, and doctors who knew Sister Bernadette, along with her letters and notes.

Sister Bernadette's Prioress at the time thought that the establishment of their monastery was justified by having produced such a soul. As a spiritual daughter of Mother Mectilde of the Blessed Sacrament (Catherine de Bar), the foundress of the Institute, Sister Bernadette grasped fully what it meant to be a sacrificial victim and responded generously to God's love, which is constantly being despised and wounded, but remains present close at hand in the Blessed Sacrament.

Sister Bernadette's sacrifice reminds us that the Church is the Mystical Body of Christ, in which those who love more, regardless of their own poverty, can make up for those who love too little or even betray that love. Not every soul is led by God as Sister Bernadette's was, but whether the soul is a candle with a steady flame or a briquette of coal which, when flared up, heats the whole world, let it love and abide in God so that in it also God may be glorified.

Mother Maria-Blandyna Michniewicz, OSBap
Prioress, Benedictine Nuns of Perpetual Adoration, Warsaw
Feast of Saint Scholastica,
10 February, 2022

*[handwritten margin note: Mystical * Body of X]*

PART 1
Biographical Sketch

Róża Wolska

1
In the Midst of the World

Family Background

The life of Sister Bernadette (Róża Maria Wolska) can be divided into three periods of different lengths. Each of them is rich, or "spacious," as she herself would call it.

The first period encompasses her childhood and youth. Róża Maria lived twenty-four years as a lay person, enjoying the beauty and joy of (1) life while facing numerous personal, familial, and national hardships.

In the second period she spent nearly the next twelve years at the Monastery of Benedictine Nuns of Perpetual Adoration of the (2) Blessed Sacrament.[1] It was here that she could fully immerse herself

---

1 The monastery of the Benedictines of Perpetual Adoration in Warsaw (Rynek Nowego Miasta 2) was founded in 1687–88 under the auspices of Queen Marie Casimire Louise de La Grange d'Arquien (1641–1716), the French wife of Jan III Sobieski. Marie Casimire had made a vow to invite Mother Mectilde's nuns to make a foundation in Poland if King Sobieski was successful in his opposition of the Turks, which victory was epitomized in his relief of Vienna in 1683. After lengthy negotiations, fourteen nuns eventually set out for Poland in 1687, braving numerous dangers of the road and sea to reach Poland. The foundation was beset by difficulties and the French nuns found it difficult to integrate with their new surroundings. One of the conditions imposed by the Queen was that the nuns run a small girl's school, although this was foreign to the contemplative orientation of their observance. The school was eventually closed in 1865 by the Tsarist government. Oppression of Catholicism resulting from the Prussian and Russian partitions had already been growing for several decades (see page 41, note 1) and in the same year the anti-Catholic government confiscated the nuns' dowries and forbade the admission of new novices—a sentence to slow extinction. The Governor-general also tried to interfere with their prioral elections, and deprived them of funds. Although their material affairs stabilized after a few years, we can only guess what suffering, hope, and surrender to God's will must have marked the nuns' lives during the following years as the community aged. Although they tried at all costs to maintain the Divine Office and Adoration, the day came when they had to give up the conventual recitation of Matins. The laity began to assist with maintaining the hours of Adoration. Relief finally came forty years later, in 1905, with Nicholas II's Edict of Toleration. New vocations began to arrive, but the gap between the

in the interior life. The development of her personality took place
in the monastery in a joyful contemplative life purchased on the
cross: "I will ... make them joyful in my house of prayer" (Is 56:7).

The final period is the time of her immolation offered in union
with Christ, "that they [the sheep] may have life, and may have it
more abundantly" (Jn 10:10). These were the last two months of her
life, crowned with eternity.

Róża Maria Wolska, affectionately known as Rozmarynka ("little
Rosemary"), came from an old family of landed gentry, bearing the
Lubicz coat of arms. The family perfectly understood the meaning
of the expression *noblesse oblige*, as evidenced by their considerable
achievements in the realms of both spiritual and material culture, as
well as their devoted service to their country. It so happened that in
this family women had been leading the way for several generations.
Karol Młodnicki, Rozmarynka's great-grandfather, was a talented
painter, who prioritized gainful employment to support his family
over the cultivation of his talent. He married Wanda Monné from a
family of French immigrants from the time of the Revolution, who
had previously been Artur Grottger's[2] fiancée. The testament to this
relationship is a series of charming portraits of Wanda along with a
collection of letters exchanged by the betrothed couple.[3]

Tragically, her fiancé died of tuberculosis before they could marry.
Grottger himself introduced her to Młodnicki, presenting him as a

---

old nuns and the newcomers made a normal religious formation very difficult.
In 1915 the Germans occupied Warsaw and looted the monastery, not even
sparing the organ pipes. After World War I, inflation forced the community
into desperate financial straits. Although they were helped by donations from
foreign monasteries of the Institute, as well as by the efforts of Dom Raymond
Thibaut of Maredsous, ecclesiastical authorities questioned the advisability of
continuing the struggling community's existence, especially due to the lack of
competent personnel. This problem was solved by the coming of Mother Janina
Byszewska (see page 41, note 1). The monastery of the Benedictine Nuns of
Perpetual Adoration in Warsaw is the longest running Perpetual Adoration
site in Poland, as well as being the only monastery of the Institute founded in
Mother Mectilde's lifetime still in existence in the same place.

2   Artur Grottger (1837–1867) was a Polish painter and graphic artist, one of
the most prominent artists of Polish romanticism, despite his premature death
at 30. Wanda Monné, whom he met in 1866, was the love of his life.

3   See *Artur i Wanda, Dzieje miłości Artura Grottgera i Wandy Monné. Listy.
Pamiętniki*, Medyka-Lwów, 1928.

Self-portrait and Portrait of Wanda Monné-Młodnickiej by Karol Młodnicki
(1835–1900), Róża's great-grandfather. (Images: Wikimedia Commons)

very noble man. Although Wanda was very happy in her marriage, she never forgot her first love and together with her husband she carefully maintained the legacy of Grottger, who in the meantime became known as the "apostle and bard" of the January Uprising.[4]

The Młodnickis' daughter, Maryla, later Wolska after her husband, belonged to a circle of famous poets of the Young Poland[5] movement. Her talent was recognized by the most celebrated among them, including Leopold Staff and Edward Porębowicz. The latter dedicated a copy of his translation of Dante's *Divine Comedy* to her, calling her in the inscription the "champion of the Polish language."

Maryla Wolska, circa 1895.
(Image: Wikimedia Commons)

---

4   The January Uprising (1863–64) was the biggest and the longest-lasting Polish insurrection. Fought against the Russian Empire, it was aimed at the restoration of the Polish-Lithuanian Commonwealth. It failed despite initial victories, and its collapse was followed by harsh reprisals, including executions, exile, and confiscation of numerous estates.

5   Young Poland (Młoda Polska) was a literary period in the history of Polish literature from 1891 to 1918.

Out of Maryla and Wacław Wolski's children, the most famous were their two daughters: Aniela Pawlikowska, a renowned portrait painter, who even painted Queen Elizabeth II's children, and Beata Obertyńska, a writer and poet, who was even more talented than her mother.

Finally, in the next generation, it was Róża Maria whose life was to be the most authoritative and relevant, albeit in ways different from those that gave recognition to her venerable aunts, grandmothers, and great-grandmothers.

She was the daughter of Kazimierz, the oldest surviving son of Wacław and Maryla Wolski, and of Anna, née Sozańska. They settled in the family estate of Perepelniki near Lviv, which one of their ancestors on the mother's side received in recognition of his participation in the Battle of Vienna of 1683.[6] The estate was considered more of a family heirloom than a source of income, and so after successive owners died, nobody thought about dividing it. The lovely estate was neglected and burdened with debt. The house, a typical Polish manor, evoked a sense of familiarity. Years later, a photograph of the house was sent to Sister Bernadette to please her. Her reaction was unexpected:

> Seeing the photo of Perepelniki was a very strange and powerful experience for me . . . . At first I thought to myself how similar the manor looked to the one in Perepelniki, and when I saw the inscription on the back, I got so emotional that I had to dry my handkerchief on the radiator.[7]

Birth of Róża Maria Wolska

The marriage of Kazimierz and Anna, née Sozańska, was blessed with many children. After Marcin (b. 1923) and Krzysztof (b. 1926), Rozmarynka was born. However, she was not born without problems. Mrs. Wolska gave the following account of the matter:

---

6   The Battle of Vienna (September 12, 1683) was fought against the Ottomans by the forces of the Holy Roman Empire led by the Habsburg Monarchy and the Polish–Lithuanian Commonwealth under the command of King John III Sobieski. Sobieski's victory is often viewed as a turning point in history, after which the Ottomans were no longer a threat for Christian Europe. The Feast of the Holy Name of Mary is celebrated on September 12 because of this battle. It was because of this victory that the Benedictines of Perpetual Adoration were invited to Poland: see page 3, note 1.

7   Letter to her mother, January 25, 1960.

The wedding of Róża's parents,
Anna, née Sozańska, and Kazimierz Wolski.

Anna Wolska before the War.

Mother was open to terminating pregnancy. Advised to

I might not have had her, because my gynecologist told me to terminate the pregnancy due to my poor health, since I had given birth to Krzysztof a year before. I did not object to this suggestion until [illegible word] my aunt Zofia Bogdanowicz, a friend of my mother's, made me aware of the moral danger of such an intervention and of the fact that it was a grave sin, and thus saved Rozmarynka. I am writing about it, because this issue is so tragically relevant today.[8]

Mrs. Wolska went to a school run by the Sisters of the Holy Family of Nazareth and was a deeply pious person, a quality which only intensified with age. In this case, however, we can see her ignorance of the moral teaching of the Church, probably due to the fact that the problem of abortion was not discussed at boarding schools run by religious sisters. She was not guilty of ill will, as evidenced by her immediate willingness to save the child even at the cost of her own life. Sister Bernadette was aware of this dark chapter of her life and knew that she owed her life to her mother in a twofold way. She wrote:

> And most of all I thank my mother for the fact that I am alive, because I might not have been, but I am, and on top of that I am HERE. I think about this very often and thank the Lord God for all these blessings, knowing that eternity will not suffice to thank Him for them and to adore Him.[9]

Mother-Daughter Bond

Rozmarynka had an exceptionally tender love for her mother. Mrs. Wolska also had a special affection, as is often the case, for this child saved from death, her first daughter, who was successful and, in many ways, similar to her mother.

The issue of the life of the unborn was always important to Sister Bernadette. When, toward the end of her life, she was at a gynecological clinic, she tried several times to save the lives of unborn children. Once she succeeded by offering material assistance from the monastery to a mother and her child. Sister Bernadette rejoiced immensely in this, as if the child were her own. Other attempts were unsuccessful.

advocate for the unborn

---

8 *Mother's Journal*, part I, p. I.
9 Letter to her mother, February 8, 1959.

Róża Maria was born on July 3, 1927, at the family villa in Lviv, which was known as Zaświecie. She was baptized in the Perepelniki chapel in mid-August. The first sacrament of Christian initiation was administered to her by a family friend, Father Dorożyński, the pastor from Olejów. Her godparents were her aunt Zofia Zawiszyna, later known as Kernowa, of Goszyce, and Mr. Głowiak, a tutor and friend of the Wolskis. Her name was chosen because of its beautiful meaning, referring to the name of the flower, the rose.

Despite the doctors' predictions, both mother and child enjoyed good health, and in the following years Mrs. Wolska gave birth to three more children: Joanna (b. 1932), Anna Genowefa (b. 1934) and Piotr (b. 1939). In addition to taking care of the growing number of children and running the house, during the year when Rozmarynka was born her mother had to take on the role of the administrator of Perepelniki, which included paying debts and taxes, since her husband had started his medical studies, which he completed with a surgeon's diploma.

Early life in Perepelniki

Despite the rundown condition of the estate, life in Perepelniki was idyllic for the children, guests, and servants. The Polish manor also had impeccable relations with the neighboring Ukrainian peasants. Rozmarynka thrived on this carefree and easygoing life. She was a charming child with flowing, waist-length blonde hair, occasionally woven into braids. She was never a beauty, but she captivated with the special charm of a tomboy. She was a very affectionate child, always longing for her parents' presence. She had barely started talking when she would exclaim, "Papa, papa!" as soon as she spotted her father walking by. It was impossible to resist this call.

Everyone was amused by her childish pronunciation, especially as she recited poems by Konopnicka.[10] At one point she was taken to Lviv to be introduced to her father's sisters. She was instructed to greet her aunts politely and kiss them. "But will they be shaved?," inquired the little one anxiously, recalling an unpleasant incident with her father.

10   Maria Konopnicka (1842–1910) was a Polish poet, novelist, children's writer, translator, journalist, critic, and activist for women's rights and for Polish independence. She is considered one of the most prominent authors in the history of Polish literature.

Rozmarynka, probably at Perepelniki.

*When her mother explained the need to control her temper,
Rozmarynka asked, "So will I always have to do that?"*

This extremely active, nimble girl was readily compared to an animal: "She was always rushing around like a young hound dog.... She climbed hazel trees like a squirrel," wrote her mother.[11] The journal makes no mention of dolls or other such toys. Rozmarynka favored living, moving creatures that could be her companions in wild play. Constant contact with nature formed the basis of her almost religious approach to it. Her father played an important role in its formation. He was a friend of a famous photographer, Włodzimierz Puchalski, whose camera captured many a secret of backcountry forests and water reeds, and who introduced children to the life of nature and taught them to listen to it.

Kazimierz Wolski loved his first daughter as dearly as did his wife. Since the feeling was reciprocal, Rozmarynka experienced the subsequent loss of her father all the more painfully. The magic of the years when she would run barefoot in the summer and ride the sleigh in a blizzard in the winter never faded for Sister Bernadette. She had two older brothers, which frequently sparks a competitive streak in an ambitious girl. When she was five or six years old, her father took her to a sheep pen and showed her a ram fight. The next day, the young girl decided to try it herself. She jumped into the sheep pen and, without a single complaint, with tears pouring down her face, she endured the angry ram's blows. Luckily, someone was passing by and saved the little girl from her predicament. On another occasion, already as an adult, she was trotting down a mountain on horseback accompanied by her father, when she got thrown off her horse. Terrified, Kazimierz returned to the scene of the accident, only to find his daughter livid with anger, wiping her boots with her riding crop and cursing at her horse. In her rage, she did not even know whether she was hurt.

However, this strong will and inexhaustible energy also had a less agreeable side. Rozmarynka's cousin, Danuta Wolska-Szczepańska, who loved her dearly, described her as "strong-willed" and a "spitfire." It was common knowledge in her household that in a fit of anger she could throw something at a person who had crossed her. She was warned that if she got too angry, a vein in her neck would rupture. Rozmarynka would then rush to the mirror and calm herself down

---

11   *Mother's Journal*, part 1, pp. 12 and 15.

after a thorough inspection of her neck. She had a particular dislike for one of her grandmothers, a noble matron with a haughty manner and an old-fashioned way of walking. Raised to respect authority figures, Rozmarynka was hardly in a position to make her dislike known. However, the lady had a dog, inseparable from the owner, which, to some extent, adopted the owner's physiognomy and gait. Once, when she found the dog alone, the girl gave it a good kicking for its "facial expression."

It was not too bad if these bouts of rage happened when she was on her own or in the presence of close family. However, the Wolskis, like all the landed gentry of those times, led a varied social life: they received guests and paid visits to their friends. Thus, their daughter had an opportunity to show what she was capable of also outside the home. Probably the best show of those abilities was given by Rozmarynka in Podlipce, at the annual name-day party of her elderly great-grandmother. The children were seated at the end of a huge table. When the hostess came up to them with a tray filled with marshmallows, Rozmarynka declared firmly, "I don't eat such disgusting things," and then, in a loud whisper, asked the girl sitting next to her, "Is that your grandma?" Upon receiving an affirmative answer, the *enfant terrible* replied with a heartfelt "Eeew!" (referring to the lady in whose honor the celebration was held, and whose kindness was matched by her ugliness). The lady of the house was laughing heartily as she was recounting the incident to the mortified Mrs. Wolska.

During the summer vacations, such "incidents" were so numerous that they warranted a special rhyming entry in the guest book: "'Rozmarynka — *enfant terribel* [sic], often tells guests: 'go to hell!'"

No wonder that on one such occasion her mother decided to have a word with her and started explaining that Rozmarynka needed to control her anger. That caught the girl's attention. Looking intently at her mother, she asked in her childish way, "So will I always have to do that?"

Her mother offered some background to justify her daughter's outbursts. Rozmarynka was ill at the time, which aggravated her hyperactivity. However, Sister Bernadette would struggle with her volatile disposition for the rest of her life. It is worth noting that although she could be impulsive and intolerable, she also exhibited natural poise.

[handwritten marginalia: "Children can mortify their parents—even future saints!" / "Gained a reputation for anger"]

Despite her challenging character, Rozmarynka was very honest. Whenever she did anything wrong, she could not keep going unperturbed. She would run through the fields with her head lowered, because she got the impression that everything around her was accusing her. The original innocence of creation and its unwavering adherence to the established laws of nature would become a personified reproach to her. *very little religious memory from her childhood.*

The lack of religious motivation in her actions and resolutions as a child is striking. The Perepelniki estate was religious in a traditional, customary way. Sister Bernadette's memories of practicing Christianity during her time at Perepelniki are scarce. She remembered and understood almost nothing from the day of her First Holy Communion. As she wrote to her mother, "Perhaps priests these days have better ways of reaching children."[12] Her mother could not even remember whether the First Holy Communion of Krzysztof and Rozmarynka took place in 1935 or 1936. The siblings were prepared for that day by the same priest who had baptized Rozmarynka, Father Dorożyński, who, according to Sister Bernadette, did not do it very well. Mrs. Wolska made a very simple white dress for her daughter and turned her own wedding veil into a First Communion veil, which was very common at that time. The children were lined up for the mandatory photograph under a blue spruce tree. During the war, Rozmarynka found this photograph and tore up the part with her likeness, which she did not care for. However, she did spare Krzysztof, who was standing next to her.

From her time at Perepelniki, Sister Bernadette also remembered the aura of her aunt, Juliuszowa Wolska, which years later she called "the atmosphere of evangelical meekness, sweetness, and simplicity."

The family separated

However, the most significant impact, although subconscious at the time, was left by reading, or rather browsing through, an illustrated Gospel book. Sister Bernadette would later confess:

> When . . . I recall my own childhood, I am increasingly convinced that nothing helps our devotion more effectively and simply than the Lord Jesus in the Gospel. Through narration

12   Letter to her mother, July 21, 1952.

contact w/ Jesus through the Gospel

and reading, a close, personal contact is established. I still remember the illustrated Gospel from Perepelniki, and I am convinced that the memory of the Lord Jesus saved me from many misfortunes. And so it continues to this day that the Gospel facilitates contact with God, and prayer.[13]

Naturally, Rozmarynka also received proper education. The year before the war started, the Wolski family moved to Lviv specifically because of the children's education. During that year, Rozmarynka attended a school run by Ursuline sisters.

The tragic September of 1939[14] came. We do not know how the girl, twelve at the time, took that national disaster. The Wolski family settled in Złoczów. In November of 1939, the father made his way to France, where he joined the Polish army that was being formed there. The family did not suffer from hunger, as the peasants from Perepelniki brought them food in horse-drawn carts almost every week. The Christmas of 1939 and the Easter of 1940 could be celebrated as if there were no war.

However, the living conditions of this large family, which had lost its natural habitat, were not easy. This is what awakened the sense of responsibility in the oldest daughter, who would mother the three younger siblings, with Piotr so little that he could not even walk yet. She started to mature imperceptibly and rapidly, relieving her mother of the burden of many activities. She didn't lose her sense of humor but acquired a seriousness and an ability to focus.

Mrs. Wolska launched successful efforts to obtain documents that would allow them to cross the Soviet-German border. Backpacks were made for the children, and although it was summer, they were dressed in winter coats, and the older three were given suitcases with everyday necessities and bundles of bedding. Mrs. Wolska's bundle was the constantly frail little Piotr. After two days spent fulfilling

---

13   Letter to her mother, January 4, 1958.

14   The Second World War started on September 1, 1939, with the German invasion of Poland. The first German attack of the war came against the Polish defenses at Westerplatte. Poland defended herself from September 1 to October 6 of 1939. Heavily outnumbered, attacked simultaneously by Germany and the Soviet Union and deserted by her allies, Poland nevertheless never signed a formal act of capitulation, and those soldiers who survived and were not taken into captivity went to France and England to keep fighting.

Róża with one of her brothers.

the formalities in Przemyśl, they found themselves on the German ~~June 16 or 24 (?) 1940~~
side and underwent disinfection. On the feast of Corpus Christi,
the Wolski family reached Cracow. A group of relatives and friends
awaited them there. First, they went to Goszyce, to their aunt Zofia
Zawiszyna. However, the house turned out to be overcrowded — up
to 30 people would stay there — so the Wolski family split up, never
to be reunited again. The mother with the sons Marcin and Piotr
stayed in Goszyce. The two younger girls, Joanna and Hania, were
taken in by the Woźniak relatives in Biórkowo. Rozmarynka and
Krzysztof were taken in by the Zubrzycki family in Wilków.

Family split up

The war years: Wilków

Róża Maria spent four formative years here and was transformed from a child into a young lady. Wilków, located about 15 miles from Cracow, was an oasis of relative calm in the midst of that part of occupied Poland that was the General Governorate for the Occupied Polish Region. Under difficult circumstances, the Zubrzycki family lived up to the tradition of Polish hospitality at its best. They took in a great number of homeless people, sharing food and clothing with them. They organized underground classes for young people of school age, in which Rozmarynka participated. She attended three grades of junior high school. Because of the advancing front, she did not manage to complete her fourth and last year of junior high school.

In Wilków, Rozmarynka experienced for the first time that which was to play such an important role in her life from that point on, namely: friendship. The daughter of the estate's owners, Hanka Zubrzycka (married name Konczewska), became her companion for study and recreation, as well as her French language teacher. Rozmarynka developed an even more affectionate relationship with her peer, Sabinka Czerniewska, also taken in by the Zubrzycki family. They were even teased a little about their ability to delight in every petal of a flower and every drop of dew. For example, Róża used to lie down in the furrows of potato fields and inhale their pungent smell with pleasure. She took every opportunity to run in the woods, ride a horse, or chase a pack of dogs, just like in Perepelniki. She was in good health; except for seasonal colds she did not suffer from any ailments. She was thin, but "healthy as a turnip," as witnesses would later attest.

The social life in Wilków offered its residents a wide range of opportunities, from bridge nights to retreats. Rozmarynka avoided shallow entertainment. She loved reading novels, especially those focusing on the psychological development of characters: *Pharaoh* by Bolesław Prus, *The Crusaders* by Zofia Kossak, *Kristin Lavransdatter* by Sigrid Undset, or *The Forsyte Saga* by John Galsworthy. Together with Sabinka, she analyzed these works and wondered about the value of books. Poetry had a privileged place in her life. Apart from reading the works of the national bards, especially Adam Mickiewicz, Róża also read the works written by members of her family, that is poems by Maryla Wolska and Beata Obertyńska. She even started writing poetry herself, but only showed her first literary attempts to a chosen few before destroying them. Most likely she felt that they did not measure up to a high enough standard. But it seems that she was, indeed, talented. Her letters read well, despite grammatical and stylistic errors.

She did, however, allow her other talents to come to fruition. Rozmarynka inherited a beautiful voice from her great-grandmother, Wanda Monné, and from her father Kazimierz, who performed successfully as a soloist. She sang in a choir as an alto, accompanied by the guitar. She happily listened to her host's piano recitals in the Wilków salon. Above all, she developed a talent for painting, inherited from her ancestors. She took painting seriously but she was also able to use it for entertainment, drawing caricatures of guests present at a party. Highly practical she learned to spin on the spinning wheel, use the sewing machine, and knit, all of which were accompanied by the simultaneous reading of books. She devoted most of her winter evenings to these activities. In the summer she played volleyball.

In Wilków, patriotic life flourished during the war. Rozmarynka, along with several other girls, took a first-aid class under the direction of Professor Stanisław Szuran and was sworn into the auxiliary units of the Home Army.[15] In the event of military operations, she would be called into service, but in the Cracow region there was no such need.

Although the family was dispersed, Rozmarynka's feelings for her loved ones did not diminish. During her stay in Wilków, she began to receive disturbing news about her father. Interned in Switzerland, Kazimierz Wolski then purchased a farm in Crouzette in central France. He tried to keep up appearances and would write to his family. Rozmarynka was probably the first one to realize the truth, when her father asked her to write a letter to the daughter of his new "acquaintance." Mrs. Wolska deluded herself the longest. Even after the end of the war she was expecting that her husband would come back or take the whole family to France. She only believed it when she had indisputable evidence that her husband was in another relationship. For Rozmarynka, perhaps more so than for the rest of her siblings, this was a huge blow. She became even closer with her mother, whose pain she shared.

---

15   Home Army (Armia Krajowa) was the name of the armed forces of the Polish Underground State during World War II.

In Wilków, during the last years of the war, the girl's religious life began to emerge. Previously, she had not been concerned about practicing her faith with any regularity. Later, she wrote to her mother,

> Twelve years ago, when I went for a horse ride with Hanka Z. in the woods and we stumbled upon an open grave with a skeleton in it, I buried my head in the sand and didn't even allow the thought that maybe God wanted to tell me something through it. I remember that it was a Sunday, and I didn't go to Luborzyca[16] because of that ride. It's horrifying to think that we can close ourselves off from God in such a way, but on the other hand, you can see looking back how His Mercy persistently chases after us in spite of everything.[17]

Programmatic disbelief was foreign to Rozmarynka, but she was no stranger to juvenile defiance and rebellion against accepted conventions, including those concerning faith. Witnesses of her stay in Wilków remember her as being torn by contradictory feelings: from adulation to contempt, from enthusiasm to resentment. Still, all of them emphasize her moral purity and nobility.

Over time, Róża's religious feelings intensified. Nature played a major part in this process. It was no longer a personified reproach to her, as it used to be in Perepelniki, but a revelation of the Creator, of His omnipotence and goodness. Although Rozmarynka was yet to turn to religious writings, she was already enchanted by the beauty of the poetry in prayers. Together with Sabinka, in the fields, she would read and analyze the Sequence to the Holy Spirit, the hymn *Veni Sancte Spiritus*, the *Trisagion*, or *Sub Tuum Praesidium*.

Wilków and the surrounding manors hosted retreats for various groups, including youth retreats. Contacts were made with the Benedictines from Tyniec,[18] thanks to which a series of retreats

---

16   A place where there was a local church and Mass was celebrated.

17   Letter to her mother, September 5, 1954.

18   The Benedictine Abbey of Tyniec, situated on the banks of the Vistula in the village of Tyniec, is thought to have been founded around 1040 by King Casimir the Restorer. Over the centuries the Abbey was destroyed several times in wars and rebuilt. In 1816 the Austrian authorities liquidated the Abbey, and in 1831 a fire lead to the Abbey being entirely abandoned. In 1939 eleven Benedictine monks from Belgium revived the Abbey, and in 1947 they began extensive restorations, such that the buildings standing today are a mix of

The Benedictine Abbey of Tyniec, situated on the banks of the Vistula, where Róża was first introduced to monastic life. (Image: Wydawnictwo Benedyktynów Tyniec)

Fr. Karol van Oost, who restored the Abbey of Tyniec and thus brought Benedictine monasticism back to life in Poland. (Image: Tyniec Abbey Archives)

was held in the manor house by the restorer of the monastery of
Tyniec and its Prior at the time, Father Karol van Oost,[19] who was
Belgian. Rozmarynka, Sabinka, and other girls also went on retreat
in Tyniec. All the evidence suggests that these retreats, perhaps
specifically those at the turn of 1943 to 1944, played a decisive role
in her life. Christ, life in God, grace — all came to her through the
Rule of the Patriarch of the West, which Bossuet called "a summary
of Christianity, a learned and mysterious abridgement of all the
teaching of the Gospel, of all the instructions of the holy fathers,
of all the counsels of perection."[20]

Living independently in Cracow

After the war ended, the new Communist authorities confiscated
the landowners' properties. Mrs. Wolska got a degree as a kindergarten
teacher and started working at a kindergarten in Nowy Sącz. Piotr
was with her. The younger boys lived separately, and the younger
girls stayed at the boarding school run by the sisters from the Congregation of the Immaculate Conception of the Blessed Virgin Mary
in Szymanów. Rozmarynka decided to become independent. She
rented rooms from families in Cracow, and her longest stay was at
Aleja Słowackiego 38. She took the classes she needed for graduating
from high school by attending adult education classes. She passed her
secondary school exit exam (*matura*) in the spring of 1947.

---

restored Gothic and Baroque architecture. Monastic life continues to flourish
there to this day, and the Abbey draws many visitors each year.

19   Fr. Karol Filip van Oost (1899–1986) was a Belgian by birth and a monk
of the Abbey of Saint Andrew in Bruges. Fr. van Oost headed the renewal of
Benedictine life in Poland and made his life's work the reopening of Tyniec
Abbey, at which he served as Prior from 1939 to 1951. He continued to follow
its development with great care even after he returned to Belgium in 1951.
Imbued with spirit of Dom Columba Marmion, in whose hands Fr. van Oost
had made his First Profession in 1918, he was distinguished by his deep sense
of community life and his charism of spiritual fatherhood. He was a born
educator and although he found mastery of the Polish language difficult, was
an author in his own right and wrote a commentary on the *Rule* of Saint Benedict. Fr. van Oost also zealously performed various apostolic labors outside
the walls of his monastery; he could be found in the salons of the aristocracy,
in the palaces of Archbishops, in seminaries, and at times serving as chaplain
to communities of women religious.

20   From the *Panégyrique de Saint Benoît*, of Jacques-Bénigne Bossuet (1627–1704).

*"Poor thing, she did everything she could
find to stay afloat," Róża's mother wrote of
her daughter's struggle in the late 1940's.*

The financial situation of the Wolski family was not easy. Fortunately, they were helped by relatives from abroad. Although Rozmarynka benefited from these care packages, she felt that they were meant for her mother and siblings rather than for her. She described the short time during which she relied solely on these for livelihood as unfair to her loved ones. The girl's resourcefulness in finding sources of income knew no limits. In 1945, Rozmarynka found a job as a laborer at Góralik's farm in the Wola Justowska district of Cracow and commuted there from downtown. In 1946, she worked in the garden of the Red Cross house on Straszewski Street. Then, together with her cousin Danuta, with whom she became very close at that time, she got a job as a waitress in the canteen of the Coal Association. For two hours of arduous service at lunchtime they received meager pay and provisions, such as leather boots and meals. Those meals from the time right after the war, flavored with rancid fat and eaten in a hurry, probably contributed to her subsequent digestive problems. Rozmarynka also worked as an extra at the theater: for example, she was an elf in *A Midsummer Night's Dream* by Shakespeare. She had to quit that job because all-day rehearsals took too much time. She knitted sweaters, worked as a typist, bought fur gloves and sold them with a profit. "Poor thing, she did everything she could find to stay afloat," wrote her mother.[21] And at the same time, she was still continuing her education.

The art student

In 1948, Róża (the student community used her proper name without the diminutive) enrolled in the four-year Higher School of Fine Arts, which at the time was a branch of the Academy of Fine Arts. After the first year, she chose graphic design at the book department as her major and became acquainted with other graphic arts disciplines. Completing numerous assignments as a student required familiarity with many disciplines and took up a lot of time. Individual work outside of school did not seem possible, but circumstances forced Róża to reconcile her studies with making a living.

At that time, the student body was very diverse in terms of age, since some were making up for the time lost during the war. Rozmarynka was one of the youngest students, which by no means left her on the periphery of social life, let alone creative life. Among artistic individuals, she was one of the strongest personalities. Her friend from the first year of her studies, Ewa Szczęk, writes, "She was extremely talented. She drew very well, had a great sense of form in painting, and was very subtle in her use of color."[22]

Although she was a novice graphic artist, her works were already being bought, for example for the 1949 exhibition in Poznań. Mrs. Wolska was particularly fond of Rozmarynka's drawing of a rather narrow, crooked street — probably Wiślna Street — at night, filled

---

21   *Mother's Journal*, part i, p. 26.
22   Letter to Sister Jadwiga Stabińska, date unclear, 1975 or 1976.

with the yellowish glow of an old-fashioned streetlamp and a drowsy moon. A small pedestrian in a red coat was walking down this street, solitary and fading into the urban landscape. The piece looked like a self-portrait of a late-night return from the theater or symphony hall. Despite extensive searching, this piece could not be located. Róża Wolska's exam piece — a portrait of a laborer — was also lost.

As a painter, she was a fan of the impressionists, especially Gauguin and van Gogh, and avant-garde modern art, particularly abstract art. Of the old masters, she valued Blessed Fra Angelico because of the subtle spirituality of his frescoes, but was rather dismissive of Raphael.

As Róża's success as a painter grew, her artistic work increasingly replaced her various odd jobs, although doing it to earn money usually meant compromising her artistic ambitions. She designed labels for bottles and boxes, and made environmentalist posters promoting nature conservation. All these odd jobs paid well and allowed her to survive financially and even help her family. As far as possible, Rozmarynka tried to spend vacations and holidays with her family.

She was able to give even more support to her mother. When Mrs. Wolska travelled at night from Nowy Sącz to Cracow for the Benedictine oblates' monthly days of recollection, Rozmarynka would invite her to her room and update her on everything that had happened with her and her siblings. They were particularly fond of the Salesian motto *tout bellement* — everything gently.

Still, Róża kept thinking about finding an apartment. This would have solved the difficult family situation, all the more so since her mother's housing arrangements in Nowy Sącz turned out to be very modest. When the hopes of her mother moving to Cracow failed in 1949, Rozmarynka encouraged her to move to Warsaw or to a place near it with money obtained from the sale of Matejko and Grottger paintings owned by the family. Her natural sense of realism, however, made her question whether the money would have covered the cost of buying a place. The idea of living in Warsaw did not pan out. It was not until early 1951 that the daughter managed to find "a classic proletarian apartment" for her mother at 26 Floriańska Street in Cracow.[23] Her siblings were slowly starting their own families and lived in their own apartments.

---

23   Letter to her mother, January 30, 1951.

The bloom of life

During her college years, Róża Wolska had a busy social life. She was universally liked for her charm, ebullience, and sense of humor, which had what the French call *esprit*, because it was both light and on point. Because of her background, her milieu included highly cultivated people. College expanded this carefully selected group. Rozmarynka's favorite friend from college was Ewa Szczęk, later Czarnocka-Januszkowska. The latter could not explain why they became so fond of each other among so many students. She gave only one valuable hint, namely that it was a spiritual friendship. Róża's room witnessed many pleasant conversations with her friends, and even more laughter. Nobody knew how to laugh as delightfully as she did, until she was out of breath. She and Ewa Szczęk were literally rolling with laughter while reading *The House at Pooh Corner* by Milne. They also discussed serious books, such as *Analysis of Happiness* by Władysław Tatarkiewicz. Róża continued to be fascinated by poetry; her favorite bard at the time was Konstanty Ildefons Gałczyński. Whenever possible, she enjoyed going to the theater, to concerts, or to painting exhibitions.

Róża was universally liked for her humor, poise, and exuberance.

Rozmarynka preferred casual and practical clothes, but she was particular about them. She rarely found anything suitable for herself in the parcels she received. She looked for unique things. Once she procured horse hide and used it to have shoes with wooden soles made for herself and Danuta. She also bought a white sheepskin coat and unusual gloves. She knew exactly how to wear her hair. She attended parties and participated in games. For her last ball where "colorful vertigo" was the theme, she made for herself a beautiful costume of Latorosłka from the novel *Bolesław Chrobry* by Antoni Gołubiew.

She had a teenage propensity to become infatuated with a man who would suddenly appear perfect to her and who, as a rule, would be unaware of the feelings he had stirred. In Wilków, the master of the house became such an ideal for her, but he treated her the way a mature man should treat a teenage girl. However, Rozmarynka did not date anyone regularly and felt no such need. As her cousin put it, she "brushed off" suggestions of such a nature from men. A healthy friendship was enough for her.

Although she was sleep-deprived and her nutrition was not optimal, Róża did not deny herself the pleasure of active recreation, namely sports, which her young and still healthy body craved. She spent Sundays and holidays taking various trips to pursue hiking, biking, motorbiking, canoeing, or skiing. During her stay in Warsaw in the summer of 1950 when she worked as an apprentice at a printing store, she brushed up on her horseriding skills at the racetracks of Służew. She developed a real love of sailing. In 1949, under the guidance of her brother, she took a sailing course in Giżycko and diligently studied sailing theory, since this was the area in which she was most lacking. Already as a postulant at the Nuns of the Blessed Sacrament, she wrote to her mother, "Please tell Marcin, as a consolation, that I often see sailboats tacking and gybing on the Vistula; it is hard for me not to think of him then."[24]

Rozmarynka also became a member of the Polish Tourist and Sightseeing Society, and as a result was able to rent equipment from the Cracow branch and explore the areas of Pilsko, Barania Góra, and Skrzyczne.[25] She considered mountaineering to be the noblest sport because of its disinterestedness and the primacy it allows for the spirit, unparalleled in other sports. Nature spoke to her again, this time as an urge to prayer. Years later, Sister Bernadette would write:

---

24 Letter to her mother, June 1, 1951.
25 Pilsko (1,557 m), in the Żywiec Beskids range, is a popular hiking and skiing destination, while Barania Góra (1,220 m) and Skrzyczne (1,257 m) are the highest peaks of the Silesian Beskids range in southern Poland.

A snapshot of Róża on a skiing expedition.

Mount Skrzyczne in winter. (Image: Levarian/CC-BY-SA-4.0/Wikimedia)

A path on the slope of Barania Góra in the Silesian Beskids.
(Jakub Hałun/CC-BY-SA-4.0/Wikimedia)

I remember Pilsko like it was yesterday. Somehow I was at the head of the group and, imagine that, I started praying spontaneously. The loneliness and those stars, and coming out of the dark forest where there might have been wolves, all that together filled me with immense gratitude towards the Lord God.[26]

However, these momentous experiences become secondary to personal models. Sister Bernadette herself writes about it as follows:

> I found ... that, in my case, if it had not been for Danusia, and certainly other people too, but especially her, the Lord God would have worked things out differently. But the fact remains that He did not want to work things out differently, and that her influence and example at that time when my "bones" were rather soft, was decisive, and I owe a lot to her.[27]

Years later, Mrs. Szczepańska (Danusia) would try to downplay the role she played: "Please do not overestimate my influence on Rozmarynka.... She was always ten times wiser and deeper than me. Later I could not keep up with her."[28]

An oblate of Tyniec

Having already been introduced to the Tyniec environment during her Wilków period, Róża Wolska became even more fully involved in it after the war. The early postwar years were a time when the Benedictine oblates in Tyniec flourished.[29] The oblates attracted,

---

26   Postscript from a letter to Ewa Januszkowska, née Czarnocka, January 16, 1958.

27   Letter to her mother, July 21, 1952. Danusia is the diminutive of Danuta.

28   Letter to Sister Jadwiga Stabińska, May 19, 1978.

29   Some notable oblates of Tyniec include Blessed Hanna Chrzanowska (1902–1974); her assistant, Alina Rumun (1924–2007), the recipient of the Florence Nightingale Medal; the Lublin psychologist Zenomena Płużek (1926–2005); Anna Świderkówna (1925–2008), a papyrologist of Egyptian and Greek sources and author of many books on the Bible; Izabela Kumelowska (1916–2008), a chemist, agriculturalist, actress, sailor, and anti-Nazi conspirator; Dariusz Waldziński (1959–2011), university professor of economics and proponent of Catholic Social Teaching; Antoni Franaszek (1922–2012), an historian, teacher, prison educator, journalist, archivist, and museum director; Ludmiła Flagorowska (1942–2012), architect and member of the Polish Academy of Sciences, with hundreds of published studies.

above all, the creative intelligentsia that in some measure set the tone for postwar Catholicism, but also young people. Several vocations to Benedictine monasteries in Poland emerged from their ranks.

The lay oblates, who belong to a particular Benedictine monastery by virtue of their promises, are an extension in the world of the monastic family of which they are members. In 1946, Father Karol von Oost entrusted the spiritual care of the laity to Father Piotr Rostworowski.[30] He was the one who led the monthly oblate days of recollection, although occasionally other fathers would fill in for him. Those days were open not only to the oblates, but also to friends of the Abbey. Rozmarynka Wolska and her mother were part of the latter group for a long time. Those days of prayer, religious reflection, discussion, and meetings with a circle of spiritually advanced people became extremely important to Róża. Years later, when writing about her confessor's visits to the monastery, Sister Bernadette used the following analogy: "It is always for me a great first-class feast, just like the oblate day used to be."[31]

Because of the challenges of getting to Tyniec (even though it was accessible by car, since few had one at the time, walking or biking was

---

30   Piotr Rostworowski (1910–1999) was the son of Elżbieta née Plater-Zyberków and Wojciech Rostworowski, a senator of the Republic of Poland. After serving in the military and pursuing secular studies in Paris, he decided to enter the Abbey of Saint Andrew in Bruges. He made his First Profession there on January 25, 1932, and was ordained to the priesthood on July 18, 1937. In 1938 he was sent by his Abbot to prepare for the return of monks to Tyniec, and his efforts culminated in the reopening of the monastery on the eve of World War II, in July 1939, where he served as novice master in the years following. From 1951–1959 he served as Tyniec's Prior, replacing Karol van Oost. Fr. Piotr's friendship was valued by numerous important ecclesiastics, from Cardinal Wyszyński to then-Bishop Wojtyła, and his influence among the Catholic intelligentsia and resistance to communism meant he was often under surveillance by the secret police. In 1966, Fr. Piotr was imprisoned for his involvement in helping two women escape to the USA, but was paroled the following year. In 1968, at the request of the undermanned Camaldolese, he took the position of the Prior of their monastery in Bielany in Cracow. He pronounced his vows as a Camaldolese in 1972, subsequently serving as Prior of various Camaldolese communities in Italy and Colombia. In his last years, he attempted to embrace an entirely eremitic form of life, but its realization was only sporadic due to ill health. Fr. Piotr contributed the translation of the Song of Songs to the Millennium Bible, and left a number of writings on theology and spirituality.

31   Letter to her mother, January 29, 1953.

Tyniec Abbey was a place where Róża and her friends could deeply experience the Mysteries of Christ — even if it was freezing! (Image: Kriksos/CC-BY-3.0/Wikimedia)

Father Piotr Rostworowski, who often led days of recollection for the oblates of Tyniec. Here he is pictured in the white habit of the Camaldoli, whom he subsequently joined. (Image: Tyniec Abbey Archives)

essentially the only option), these days usually took place in Cracow, in an apartment of one of the oblates. They started with Low Mass. At the beginning of the day, the oblates recited Prime,[32] and the day ended with the recitation of Compline. The presiding Father gave two conferences. The first was a commentary on a chapter of the *Rule* of Saint Benedict, while the second was an introduction to Scripture or a commentary on selected liturgical questions. Attendance was not mandatory, but the oblates and friends rarely missed the meetings. Tyniec gave them that which brought renewal in the Church at the time: love for the Holy Eucharist, the liturgy, and the Sacred Scriptures (at least fifteen minutes of daily *lectio divina* was recommended). In addition to the *Rule*, that is, the "law" under which the oblate, like the monk, wanted to "fight,"[33] the oblates would exchange books by various Benedictine authors, especially the well-known trilogy by Blessed Columba Marmion: *Christ in His Mysteries*; *Christ, the Life of the Soul*; and *Christ, the Ideal of the Monk*.[34] Many of the oblates, especially the young ones, attended religious education classes that were available in Cracow at that time.

---

32 One of the seven "day hours" of the Monastic Office, and more specifically, the one that marks the beginning of the workday. Although suppressed by the Second Vatican Council in the Roman Breviary (*Sacrosanctum concilium* 89d), the office of Prime has remained in use to this day among some clergy, religious communities, and laity.

33 See the *Rule* of Saint Benedict, ch. 58.

34 Blessed Columba Marmion (1858–1923) was born Joseph Aloysius Marmion in Dublin, Ireland. Ordained a priest for the Archdiocese of Dublin, he subsequently discerned a call to the monastic life and entered the Beuronese Abbey of Maredsous in Belgium. After profession, he served as assistant novice master at his monastery, and in 1899 was appointed Prior of Maredsous's newly founded house of studies, Mont César in Louvain, where he taught theology to the young monks. He became widely regarded as a retreat master and traveled across western Europe serving religious communities of all orders in this capacity. In 1909 he was elected Abbot of Maredsous, and consequently returned to the monastery of his profession. He adopted as his motto *Magis prodesse quam praesse*, "To serve rather than be served," taken from Saint Benedict's description of how an Abbot ought to govern. As Abbot he had to shoulder the burden of governing a community of a hundred monks and a monastery which ran a boarding school, a school of fine arts, and a publishing house renowned for its production of *La Revue Bénédictine*. During the Great War, Abbot Marmion took many of his young monks to a refuge in Ireland to protect them from conscription. His trilogy mentioned in the text were books based on retreat talks he

"I was only filled with some 'great need' that pushed me here,"
Sister Bernadette later recalled of the time leading up to her entrance.

The oblates were encouraged to find a regular confessor, preferably a Benedictine, but it was not absolutely required. When participating in the oblate days of recollection, Róża Wolska sometimes, although not always, went to confession with Father Piotr. She never asked him for spiritual direction: this relationship emerged spontaneously. He became the only spiritual director she had in her life, although out of necessity she would go to confession with other priests more frequently. She was never a difficult penitent. In fact, she hardly had any problems. She was not one of those people who torture their confessors with long conversations or lengthy letters; even in the cloister, she hardly wrote to him. She was one of those souls who, as Dom Marmion put it, while living with the Church, the liturgy, and the Scriptures, allow themselves to be led by the Church and therefore need individual direction much less.

The formative influence of Tyniec on the deepening of Róża's interior life included her experience of religious feasts there, especially those of Holy Week. Those were truly days of great spiritual intensity for her. And yet the difficult postwar conditions were probably not conducive to this. It seems that Rozmarynka spent Holy Week in Tyniec with Danusia on two different occasions. The girls usually walked from Cracow with their own provisions, because all they got at the monastery was soup for dinner. They lived in the countryside. They were not dressed warmly enough for the weather. The cold in the church was a deterrent, but the greatness of the mystery of Christ unfolding there attracted them. They did not miss a single one of the many-hour-long services. Wonderful texts, Gregorian chant, trained voices, refined liturgical vestments — all this was not just a spiritual feast, but also an aesthetic one. After the liturgy, the girls, freezing with cold, would leave the church and soak up the spring sun, whenever it was out. Though cold and hungry, they were perfectly happy, because they were satisfied with the experience of Christ's mystery.

---

gave and became extremely popular, receiving praise from Benedict XV, Pius XI, Pius XII, Paul VI, and John Paul II. They were translated into many languages, including Korean and Japanese. They had already been translated into Polish by the year of Róża Wolska's birth. His teaching was enriched by Sacred Scripture and an emphasis on the liturgical life of the Church, and focused especially on the themes of divine adoption and likeness to Christ as keys to the spiritual life. He was beatified by Pope John Paul II on September 3, 2000.

As far as possible, Rozmarynka visited Tyniec on other feast days as well. Corpus Christi used to be celebrated there with particular solemnity. The procession circled around almost the entire village. Róża took part in these celebrations together with Ewa Szczęk. On a hot June day, Ewa wanted to seek relief from the sun in the shade of the linden trees, but Róża explained to her that the whole point of the procession was that it was hot, that people were thirsty, and that they were really exhausted. "Well, and so I persevered. I often remind myself of this when I am greatly troubled and literally collapse from my worries."[35]

Her formal affiliation with Tyniec took place on June 24, 1949 when she began the oblate novitiate. At the vestition, Róża Wolska chose the name Bernadette after the visionary from Lourdes, Saint Bernadette Soubirous. She always had a special love for this saint because of her humility and simplicity, her hidden life filled with suffering, and a certain similarity of character in terms of her sense of humor and her abrasive personality. She made her oblate profession on December 8, 1950.

A deepening awareness of God

More and more, God's fullness in Róża's life was revealing itself. Jan Józef Szczepański gave a beautiful testimony to this in his article "Japanese Flowers" (printed in the April 1977 issue of the *Kultura*[36] magazine). There he writes about an occasional haunting sensation of reality, of participation in an existence which cannot be taken away, and of accompanying factors such as "water, cold, radiance, the crispness of mountain air, a feeling of lightness." He describes a return from some Tatra climbing, already at night, in deep silence. Just below, a pond with drowning stars was shining, as if retreating from the wanderer rather than getting closer, while the outlines of the ridge overhead marked, as it were, the final border of being. Finally, leaning over the water receding steadily into the distance, he submerged his face in its clear depth, and bitterly confessed his inability to take advantage of these moments of blessing. Jan Józef Szczepański concludes:

---

35   Letter to Sister Jadwiga Stabińska, April 4, 1977.
36   *Kultura* (*Culture*) was a leading Polish-émigré literary-political magazine, published from 1947 to 2000.

I never attempted to have this story printed, and I never showed it to anyone except Danusia and Róża, two girls whose affection was very important to me at the time. I recall that evening in a sub-let room, in the yellow glow of a standing lamp. The two girls were on the couch—Danusia, dark and swarthy, with her brow furrowed, and Róża, pale, with a cheerful face, perched on her bent legs, as if ready to jump up at any moment and run somewhere laughing. And on the chair under the lamp, in my lap, a freshly finished manuscript, rustling gently in my hands, which shook slightly with excitement. I was reading, and the words were growing in my mouth. There were too many of them. I choked on them, I felt my cheeks burning, and the silence of my listeners filled me with the worst feelings, so when I reached the end, I did not dare to raise my eyes from the sheets of paper, nor did I dare ask any questions for fear of hearing some perfunctory compliment that would definitively seal my defeat. And then that which I least expected happened. After a long moment of silence, Róża said something, I don't remember exactly what. Perhaps it was a mere "thank you," or perhaps something more, but the sound of her voice, the way in which she uttered those few words, proved with all certainty that she had grasped that which I could not express or even understand, which I was seeking awkwardly and in the dark. And my embarrassment became even deeper, for I already knew that I had missed everything, that I had failed to draw any conclusions from my vague experiences, that I had not approached any reality, but had only avoided it by making clever faces, and yet my blank check was accepted in good faith by someone who had the means to cover it.

The first thought of an exclusive commitment to God occurred to Rozmarynka after a sermon by Father Karol Wojtyła,[37] then a vicar at Saint Florian's Church, which was part of a series of May reflections on the book by Saint Louis Marie de Montfort, *True Devotion to Mary*. Soon after, Rozmarynka hesitantly mentioned her vocation to Father Piotr. "I told her firmly that she had a vocation.

---

37 Karol Wojtyła later became Pope John Paul II. He was a vicar at the Parish of Saint Florian in Cracow from 1949 to 1951. He was familiar with the Tyniec community, having first visited there as a seminarian.

As a rule, I avoid putting things this way, but this time I saw it so clearly that I had no doubts."[38]

Her daughter's decision to enter the monastery was a blow to Mrs. Wolska, who counted on her material help. However, having a deep faith herself, she quickly came to terms with this fact. Rozmarynka's father gave her a sorrowful but permissive and affectionate response when she was already at the monastery. Other relatives and loved ones came to terms with her decision later or not at all, although she presented it to them as a way to help the world by constant prayer.

In January of 1951, Róża Wolska was hospitalized for the first time and spent six weeks in the hospital. Tests revealed mild jaundice and higher than normal levels of stomach acid. Later it turned out that there were some complications.

It was Father Piotr who suggested to her the Monastery of the Benedictine Nuns of Perpetual Adoration of the Blessed Sacrament. She visited them for the first time in 1950. In 1951, upon her release from the hospital, she went there for a "fundamental conversation." The Novice Mistress, Mother Celestyna Wielowieyska,[39] openly told her that she would not be able to do art with a capital "A" in the monastery. She heard in reply, "That is not necessary at all. I

---

38   Letter to Sister Jadwiga Stabińska, Easter of 1976.

39   Mother Maria Celestyna of the Sweetest Heart of Jesus (Maryla Wielow-ieyska, 1902–1968) came from a noble family of the Półkozic coat of arms. She led an ordinary life of a girl from a good home and, in 1927, although not without some hesitation, she entered the Carmelite monastery in Lviv. She stayed there for two years but left for reasons of health. When her health improved, she joined the Benedictine Nuns of Perpetual Adoration of the Blessed Sacrament in Warsaw in 1930, where she made her Solemn Profession in 1934. During the Warsaw Uprising, following the example of other sisters, but guided primarily by a sense of duty, she asked Mother Prioress Janina Byszewska for permission to make a private vow of sacrificing her life so that Poland would belong to Christ. However, the permission was not granted. Mother Byszewska foresaw that God was preparing Celestyna for the task of rebuilding the monastery after the war. Between 1945 and 1951, Mother Celestyna was the Novice Mistress and the Prioress's right hand, and after Mother Byszewska died, she herself was elected Prioress, a position she held from 1951 to 1967. Mother Celestyna was truly dedicated to the task of rebuilding the monastery and oversaw the founding of the monastery in Siedlce in 1959. She cultivated a rich inner life and was considered a mystic, dying on October 12, 1968, after a long and difficult illness.

want to be all His and do what [He] wants."[40] Thus, the day of her admission and other details were arranged.

Upon her return to Cracow, Rozmarynka gave away her personal belongings, including her books. Her family bought her a ticket in the sleeper car and accompanied her to the train station on the evening of May 9, 1951. That was her exodus night, her Passover: "And this day shall be for a memorial to you: and you shall keep it a feast to the Lord in your generations with an everlasting observance" (Ex 12:14).

Sister Bernadette of the Cross

2
Monastic Life

First steps

Sister Bernadette once called monastic life "a great adventure." For Miss Wolska it started in the same way as it does for other candidates. Most likely the day after her arrival she received the mandatory postulant attire. The sisters laughed at the bangs sticking out from under the bonnet, and she laughed with them. At the beginning of her religious life, the Prioress, Mother Janina Jadwiga Byszewska,[1]

---

1   Mother Janina of the Eucharistic Heart of Jesus (1886–1951) was born Jadwiga Byszewska in the village of Dzieduszyce. Despite opposition from her family, she entered the Benedictine monastery in Staniątki on November 1, 1910, and made her profession on November 13, 1912. Her life was characterized by a love of the Benedictine spirit and a fondness for Benedictine devotion to the Sacred Heart. The Monastery of Staniątki was founded sometime before 1228 by Klemens Jaksa Gryfita Wizenna. The successive Partitions of Poland by the Habsburg Monarchy, the Kingdom of Prussia, and the Russian empire at the end of the 18th century included suppression of many religious houses or governmental limitation on the number of religious allowed in any one community. However, Staniątki was the only one in the Austrian partition that avoided the numerical limitation, and thus in the twentieth century it was one of the strongest remaining communities. Consequently, Staniątki was experiencing a "golden age" by the 1920s, and in 1927 Mother Janina was able to go to Warsaw to assist the floundering community of the Benedictines of Perpetual Adoration. Although she was not enthusiastic about the difficult office entrusted to her, she quickly grew attached to the house. Fr. Karol van Oost called her "the last of the great reforming Prioresses."
    The condition of the monastery at the time meant that she ruled *manu forti* (with a strong hand), and while generous to the older sisters who had been brought up in different conditions, she was very demanding of the young vocations. Such was the number of vocations (in one year alone, the noviciate numbered fourteen) that in the years before the war a new foundation was considered. The community flourished under Mother Janina, who also oversaw extensive renovations of the Warsaw monastery for its 250-year anniversary (1688–1938); she modernized the host-making facilities of the community, first from coal fireplaces to gas, and then to electric. Under her leadership, the monastery became a center of beauty and piety in Warsaw. It was Mother

told her something that greatly influenced Sister Bernadette's monastic future: "No man putting his hand to the plough, and looking back, is fit for the kingdom of God" (Lk 9:62).

The sisters immediately sensed a choleric in Rozmarynka, someone uncompromising and full of enthusiasm for the new life. Nothing surprised her, nothing discouraged her.

May of 1951 was cold and rainy. Almost in the very first days of her stay at the monastery, Rozmarynka fell ill. The doctor suspected scarlet fever, but it turned out to be just tonsillitis which affected the joints. After attempting to take up her religious duties with no success, the postulant had to return to the hospital in June. "Actually, I am yet to begin my regular postulancy," she wrote to her mother.[2] Her continuous illnesses, especially given the difficult financial situation of the monastery at the time, made her admission uncertain. At one point Mother Byszewska even decided to send her home. However, she granted her request to extend the trial period by a few months. Her fellow sisters from the novitiate (at that time, almost the whole community consisted of novices) were very emotional about Rozmarynka's uncertain future. Her strength at the time was in accepting God's will and in trusting Him unreservedly.

The community lost its Prioress on October 18, 1951, when Mother Byszewska died, and Mother Celestyna Wielowieyska became Prioress. As it happened, she was the only Prioress Sister Bernadette had during her entire religious life and she was wholeheartedly devoted to Sister Bernadette. In the meantime, the postulant's health improved to some extent, and she was accepted to the next stage of her religious training: the canonical novitiate.

Janina who saw the community through World War II, and supported the resistance during the Warsaw Uprising by not abandoning the monastery. She headed the surviving ten sisters after nearly the whole community was killed on August 31, 1944, and presided over the beginning of the reconstruction work once the war was finished.

In the year of her death, on June 4, 1951, Mother Janina transferred her stability to Warsaw, and took the vow of Perpetual Adoration that made her a full member of the Benedictines of Perpetual Adoration. At the end of her life, she took so little food that she was almost living miraculously. She died after a wonderful ecstasy, her face radiant, and with the joyful exclamation: "All of heaven is waiting for me."

2   Letter to her mother, July 19, 1951.

Top: *The monastery before the War.* Middle: *After the Uprising of 1944.* Bottom: *Reconstruction following the war.*

The monastery church today. (Image: LoMit/CC-BY-SA-4.0/Wikimedia Commons)

*Mother Celestyna Wielowieyska in a photo taken
sometime before the 1944 Uprising.*

At that time, vestition was an extremely solemn public act.[3] On the day of Sister Bernadette's vestition, that is December 3, 1951, there was great commotion in the monastery. The postulant was dressed in a wedding gown, or rather, the silk arranged in soft pleats was pinned on her. Looking at all the white, Sister Bernadette remarked: "whited sepulchres" (cf. Mt 23:27). A multitude of guests had arrived, and they were awaiting the celebrant — in vain. Due to a misunderstanding, Father Piotr Rostworowski was convinced that the ceremony would take place in the afternoon, which is why he was so late. In the general confusion, the postulant remained calm and retired to her cell so as not to lose the focus of the retreat. With the Prioress's permission, she kept her oblate name Bernadette, and Father Piotr added to it the title "of the Cross." He said that it "sounded right to him." Although she earlier had expressed her desire to be "of God's Will," she accepted the new life-motto with fervor. The celebration was combined with Vespers, after which the sisters sang *Rorate caeli*, one of the most beautiful Gregorian chants. The ceremony was very moving and solemn.

The time in the novitiate proved to be extremely difficult for Sister Bernadette. She would receive increasingly penetrating, almost crushing insights into her spiritual wretchedness, and God was hidden. Often, she would come to the Mistress of Novices with her eyes full of tears, "Where is He? Where has He gone? I cannot live without Him." Reassured that He would return after testing her faithfulness, her eyes would light up with flashes of anticipated happiness.

It was then that Sister Bernadette described the state of a soul in the order as "enduring God." The Mistress liked this term very much and, with the novice's consent, repeated it to the other sisters. It referred to the following verse: *Confortetur cor tuum et sustine*

---

3   Today, the beginning of the novitiate, marked by vestition in the Benedictine habit, is often a simple ceremony carried out within the monastic family, without the participation of people from outside the monastery. Sister Bernadette's vestition, following the custom of the time, was a solemn rite witnessed by the novice's family, friends, and invited guests. This solemn clothing ceremony where the novice dresses as a bride is still observed in some communities. In the Polish monasteries of Perpetual Adoration this custom continues, but is now observed at the First Profession.

Dominum, "Let thy heart take courage, and wait thou for the Lord" (Ps 26:14)—literally, "endure" the Lord. In her breviary, Sister Bernadette placed a bookmark with the words of the foundress of the Institute of the Benedictine Nuns of Perpetual Adoration of the Blessed Sacrament, Mectilde of the Blessed Sacrament: "To be a victim is to accept every tribulation."[4]

---

4   Catherine de Bar was born at Saint-Dié, Lorraine, in north-eastern France, on 31 December 1614, the third child of Jean and Marguerite de Guillon de Bar. Belonging to an ancient family of magistrates, Catherine was carefully educated for life among distinguished society. However, having felt a call to the religious life from a young age, she was allowed by her father to enter the convent of the Annonciades of Bruyères shortly before she turned seventeen.

In 1635, after four years in the cloister, Mother de Bar and the other nuns were forced to flee in the face of hostilities due to the Thirty Years' War. Catherine de Bar eventually found shelter with the Benedictines in Rambervillers, her first contact with Benedictine monasticism. As a Benedictine, she took the name Mectilde after the medieval mystic Saint Mechtilde of Hackeborn. In 1654, helped by the Queen, Anne of Austria, and counselled by the Benedictine monks of the Maurist Abbey of Saint-Germain-des-Prés, Mother Mectilde began in Paris the Institute of the Benedictine Nuns of Perpetual Adoration of the Most Holy Sacrament of the Altar. Living in the midst of France's *grand siècle,* Mother Mectilde found friends and supporters among such figures as Saint Vincent de Paul, Saint John Eudes, and Jean de Bernières, while at the same time providing spiritual counsel to men and women in every state of life. In her teaching and writing, Mother Mectilde was able to synthesize in a unique way the monastic, liturgical, and ascetical traditions with much of the spirituality and mysticism which flourished among her contemporaries. By her death in 1698, Mother Mectilde had overseen the foundation of seven houses of her Institute. Although sometimes called "foundress" of the Institute, she is called in French the *institutrice* to distinguish her role from that of Saint Benedict.

Over the centuries, communities sprang up in many countries, including Italy, Germany, Poland, and the Netherlands. Today, the Benedictines of Perpetual Adoration are one of the oldest continuously surviving monastic reforms in the Church. In 2012, Silverstream Priory became the first community of men to follow the Mectildian charism, and as such received definitive approval from the Holy See in 2017. Mother Mectilde's English speaking progeny includes monks, nuns, and lay oblates across Ireland, Great Britain, the United States, the Netherlands, Uganda, and Kenya.

Mother Mectilde of the Blessed Sacrament.
(Image: Benedictine Nuns of Perpetual Adoration, Wrocław)

Art in the monastery

A painful experience in the first years of Sister Bernadette's monastic life was the problem of using her artistic talents as a painter. After the tragic bombing of August 31, 1944,[5] rebuilding the monastery was an arduous task. The nuns lived in great poverty because they had to spend every penny they earned on construction. They had to accept any job they could get their hands on. And it was the beginning of the fifties, when outside of Tyniec hardly anyone dreamt about liturgical reforms, while in the parishes the notorious Sulpician aesthetic was rampant. It originated in the 19th century, in the religious and artistic circles connected with the quarter called Saint-Sulpice in Paris, and was famous for its saccharine depictions, most of which are synonymous with religious kitsch today. This was the environment into which Róża Wolska, a lover of the avant-garde, entered. No wonder that her first attempts at demonstrating her talent in the realm of the art she had practiced were less than successful.

For the Feast of the Assumption of the Blessed Virgin Mary, August 15 of 1951, the first anniversary of the promulgation of this truth of faith as dogma, she painted the Mother of God, a painting that did not find favor in the eyes of Mother Byszewska. The Prioress criticized it as a "bald Madonna" and asked that it be repainted. When Sister Bernadette placed illustrations of the mysteries of the Rosary around the Holy Sepulcher, she was told that it looked like a newsstand filled with postcards. At least some of the nuns in the monastery liked her drawings and pictures.

Commissions of paintings for churches were even more challenging. One had to conform to the clients' tastes, or else they would not accept the work. Sister Bernadette understood that (after all, during her studies she had to undertake work that did not necessarily reflect her artistic potential), but it still did not diminish her suffering. There was something subtle and pristine in the faces she painted, but when she was doing commission work, she had to erase every mark of individuality. "It seems to me that I am sinning against the Holy Spirit," she

---

5   The monastery in Warsaw was bombed by the Germans during the Warsaw Uprising on August 31, 1944. The building was completely destroyed, with many casualties: 34 nuns, 4 priests, and around 1,000 civilians, including children, who had sought shelter at the monastery.

Linocuts of Saints Benedict and Scholastica by Sister Bernadette. The originals are quite small, approximately 2 1/4th by 4 1/3rd inches.

confided to a Benedictine nun with whom she was close. The sisters still remember how she would paint with her lips clenched, with an expression of a sorrowful grievance in her eyes, clutching her brush, as if it was an instrument of torture. Sometimes she tried to tackle this problem with her sense of humor. For example, she described to her mother that she was painting a picture of Saint Florian, and that those commissioning it cared most about the water bucket![6] "It is very good for me to conform to the firemen's taste for a bit."[7] And such commissions were many. After several years of violating her own artistic personality, something changed in Sister Bernadette. She used to say with a smile that she got used to painting "beautiful faces." With time she started to receive commissions which were about

---

6   As the patron saint of firemen, Saint Florian is usually depicted holding a bucket of water.

7   Letter to her mother, February 26, 1952, and May 9, 1952.

This drawing of Saint Benedict's and Saint Scholastica's last meeting demonstrates that Sister Bernadette was fully capable of more three-dimensional art.

HILAREM ĐATOREM ĐILIGIT DEUS.

Reg. c. V.

"God loveth a cheerful giver" (2 Cor 9:7). Used by Saint Benedict
in his Rule's chapter on obedience, this phrase characterizes well
Sister Bernadette's selfless attitude towards her artistic talents.

JAK MIŁE JEST MIESZKANIE TWOJE PANIE

"How lovely are thy tabernacles, O Lord of hosts!" (Ps 83:2).

true artistry—she painted for the Society of Friends of the Catholic University of Lublin, the Catholic Intelligentsia Club in Warsaw, and so on. She called such projects "very pleasant graphic work,"[8] yet she was no longer as drawn to such work as she once was. This does not change the fact that, during her initial novitiate stage, painting was a torment for Róża Wolska and a test of her heroic obedience. The professors at the academy were right when they predicted that she would waste her talent, and only a small number of her works have survived to this day. Nevertheless, Sister Bernadette did something incomparably greater: she painted her holiness.

Simple and Solemn Professions

During the novitiate period, the young sister's health required following a strict diet, since she suffered pain from gallstones. Despite the cost of treatment, the community did not hesitate to admit her to vows, seeing her good will and the authentic nature of her contemplative vocation. Sister Bernadette took her temporary vows on December 8, 1952, with Mass celebrated by one of the Benedictine Fathers. She summed up her experience succinctly to her cousin: "Let me tell you—it is good to take vows!"[9]

She continued in the novitiate. The three-year period before her final consecration to God through Solemn Profession was marked by consolations in her interior life and an increasingly close attention to the Scriptures.

Three years after her initial vows, on August 4, 1955, Sister Bernadette underwent gallbladder surgery. Even then she longed for God very much. On her way to the hospital run by Sisters of Saint Elizabeth, she asked Mother Prioress if she could pray to God for death. However, she sent a note from the hospital saying that she was only asking that God's will be done, "because it is probably less selfish."[10] The desire to surrender her life was running through her subconscious, for, waking from anesthesia, she said to the nurse attending to her, "The trip didn't work out; you're going to go on my ticket!" As she explained later, she meant a missed trip to heaven. Sister Bernadette

---

8   Letter to her mother, December 17, 1961.
9   Letter to Danuta Szczepańska, January 19, 1953.
10 *Journals of Mother Celestyna Wielowieyska.*

W Imię Trójcy Przenajświętszej Ojca i Syna i Ducha Św.

Ja, siostra Maria Bernadeta od Krzyża, upadając pokornie do stóp uwielbionego Stwórcy mego Jezusa Chrystusa, który jako wiarą rzeczywiście jest obecny w Boskiej Eucharystii, ślubuję i przyrzekam na całe życie, ubóstwo i posłuszeństwo według Reguły Chwalebnego Ojca naszego św. Benedykta i z wielką wdzięcznością utrzymując nieustający adorację Najśw. Sakramentu Ołtarza, zgodnie z korzystającemu na świętego Ślubowu, potwierdzanym przez Stolicę Apostolską, jako ofiara poświęcona całego jego, celem wynagradzania krzywdzących popełnianych przeciw tej Boskiej Tajemnicy. W dowód czego podpisałam to moje obecne przyrzeczenie, na wieczną chwałę Boga, na cześć Bogarodzicy Dziewicy i pod Jej szczególną opieką, na cześć wszystkich Świętych, a zwłaszcza tych, których relikwie znajdują się w tym klasztorze, wobec naszej Przewielebnej Matki Przeoryszej i całego Zgromadzenia.

dnia 10. miesiąca grudnia 1955 r.

s. Maria Bernadeta od Krzyża

Zakona w imieniu Róża Maria Uokko

s. M. Placydia od starsza siostra przeorysza

Sister Bernadette's Solemn Profession chart.

was remembered with the greatest fondness by everyone at the hospital, thanks to the aura of warmth, prayer, and kindness that she radiated. She also received much kindness herself.

Admitted to Solemn Profession after her return from treatment, Sister Bernadette took her solemn vows on December 10, 1955, because Father Piotr was unable to come on the Feast of the Immaculate Conception. In his homily, he said that all those who think that entering a cloistered monastery is an escape from the difficulties of life are wrong, as it is there that one must wrestle with Satan and experience spiritual warfare. He also said, referring to the Gospel parable (cf. Mt 25:14–30), that the talent offered on the altar is not hidden in the earth. Sister Bernadette called the retreat before her Solemn Profession an encounter with God "face to face" in the darkness of faith.[11] She encapsulated all the feelings of her heart overflowing with gratitude in one sentence, pregnant with meaning: "God is very good."[12] She completed the novitiate on the Feast of Pentecost in 1956.[13] From then on, she was a full member of the community.

Following Pope Pius XII's Apostolic Constitution *Sponsa Christi* (November 21, 1950), many monasteries of Benedictine nuns, inspired by the restoration of the *Consecratio Virginum* (Consecration of Virgins) by Abbot Guéranger for the nuns of Sainte-Cécile of Solesmes, France, in 1868, welcomed the revival of the ancient rite dating back to the fourth century. After the Second World War, the professed Benedictine Nuns of Perpetual Adoration of the Blessed Sacrament were able to avail themselves of the privilege of the consecration of virgins. It was conferred on Sister Bernadette and some of her fellow sisters by the Auxiliary Bishop of Warsaw, Jerzy Modzelewski, on the Second Sunday of Easter, April 14, 1959.

Like the other nuns, Sister Bernadette prepared for this rite by spending the day in prayer and recollection. In the evening she told Mother Celestyna, "God is preparing great graces for me, it's fantastic."

---

11   Ibid.

12   Letter to her mother, December 18, 1955.

13   According to the constitutions of the Benedictines of Perpetual Adoration then in use, sisters remained under the tutelage of the Novice Mistress for a year after their solemn vows. Although the exact arrangement has varied over time and from monastery to monastery, this practice of junior religious remaining in the "novitiate" is still a universal practice.

Cardinal Wyszyński presides at the first Consecration of Virgins at Sister Bernadette's monastery on 1 November, 1952. Sister Bernadette would receive her consecration on the Second Sunday of Easter, April 14, 1959, at the hands of the Auxiliary Bishop Jerzy Modzelewski.

After the rite, families and friends were hosted at the monastery. Sister Bernadette looked radiant in her Benedictine choir dress, the cuculla, wearing a wreath of white hyacinths over a black veil and a nuptial ring on her finger. "It is an incredible honor to wear a ring in religious life."[14] It was as if God himself, "a clear lake," was peering through her gaze, according to one of the sisters.

In the evening, Sister Bernadette slipped into the Prioress's cell: "Mother, I just had my real nuptials." And, sensing Mother Celestyna's emotion, Sister Bernadette added, "But not the mystical kind according to Saint John of the Cross, it just happened like that. He is all mine, and I am all His. It's fantastic. I'm in heaven." And in a quiet whisper, she added, "It won't be long now." Mother Celestyna shuddered and looked at her with concern, which made her visibly sad. "I thought you really loved me and would rejoice with me."[15]

14   Letter to Aunt Beata Obertyńska, June 23, 1957.
15   *Journals of Mother Celestyna Wielowieyska.*

God is truly Sr. Bernadette's Beloved

i kind of love the simplicity + accessibility of this

Immersion in the monastic tradition

Sister Bernadette was never interested in the theology of mystical states. In her inner life we find no visions, ecstasies, inner voices, or charismatic graces. It was a normal contemplative life, purchased at the price of the cross — the development of theological virtues of faith, hope, charity, and the gifts of the Holy Spirit. According to Father Piotr, her spirituality, thoroughly Benedictine, was found between the two poles of adoration and humiliation. This is a purely practical distinction, because "they honour him most that most keep humility" (Sir 3:21, Knox).

Adoration finds its first expression in the liturgical life of the Church. According to Saint Benedict, a monk should not place anything before the Divine Office, that is, the liturgical service offered to the Lord.[16] The *opus Dei* finds its complement in *lectio divina*, a reverent reading of Sacred Scripture and of the writings of the Fathers and of the saints.

Sister Bernadette prepared conscientiously for the Office. She considered her participation in it an honor, especially the function of the so-called hebdomadarian, i.e., the sister presiding over the Office in the name of the Church for a given week (*hebdomada* is Latin for "week"). During the Office, she would separate herself from external matters, infinitely less important than the God whose praises she was singing. She loved Gregorian chant so much that sometimes, when she felt unwell and had to meditate in her cell, she would open the chant books and hum the melodies from them because they inspired her to contemplation. The year, with its seemingly repetitive cycle of liturgical seasons, feasts, and solemnities, constantly dazzled her with new meaning. She used to say that she was never able to fully comprehend the mysteries of Christ, which reached their peak (as the Church believed, and so did she) in the most beautiful, most significant moment of the liturgical year: the Paschal Vigil.

For Sister Bernadette, her daily participation in the Holy Mass was a reenactment of Christ's mystery accomplished in the Paschal Triduum. She once told her superior, "Holy Mass — it is my everything, my strength and my life; without it, I feel like a parched

---

16   Cf. *Rule* of Saint Benedict, ch. 43.

desert."[17] After Holy Communion, tears would often run down
Sister Bernadette's face. vulnerable , intimate
She rejoiced in the fact that as a Benedictine Nun of Perpetual
Adoration of the Blessed Sacrament she was a very special devotee
of the Real Presence. She often said how beautiful adoration was,
abiding face to face with Jesus. She missed this form of prayer
greatly during her illnesses. After an unfortunate attempt to kneel
for a whole hour, which resulted in knee problems, she would adore
sitting on a small stool or in a choir stall, with reverence and focus.
When she once allowed herself (in her judgment) to become distracted during adoration, she asked the Prioress for permission to
do it over again.

Mother Mectilde wanted the adoration of her daughters to
become "adoration at every moment," that is, adoration embracing
one's whole life, and Sister Bernadette followed the same intuition.[18]
For one of the celebrations in the monastery, she painted the following decoration: an inscription was rising from the globe towards the
Holy Trinity: *Habemus ad Dominum*.[19] This composition appealed
to all the Benedictine nuns.

Spiritual traits

Sister Bernadette did not overemphasize reading. She once told a
sister who could not read because of an eye disease that she would
receive everything "from the roof,"[20] that is, directly from God. However, she did not fall into the other extreme of neglecting reading. She
used to say that the things she had read were very helpful during
Adoration. Following the monastic tradition, she gave priority to
the Bible, "the monk's manual for the inner life." She did not live to

---

17   Cf. Ps 62: 2; *Journals of Mother Celestyna Wielowieyska.*
18   It is difficult to say how much Sister Bernadette had read of Mother
Mectilde. Although a concerted effort to publish Mother Mectilde's writings did
not bear fruit until after the 1950's, handmade copies and original manuscripts
of her writings in French transmitted her teachings in the monastery. Sister
Bernadette knew at least some French before she entered the monastery, where
it was also taught and used to some extent (see, for example, her comments
in the letter of January 15, 1961, to her aunt Beata Obertyńska).
19   We lift them (our hearts) up to the Lord.
20   Although one might expect 'from above', this is the literal meaning of the
similarly idiosyncratic phrase in Polish.

see the publication of the Millennium Bible.[21] Like all nuns, she owned a copy of the New Testament translated from the Vulgate by Father Eugeniusz Dąbrowski. She also used the translation of the New Testament from Greek by Father Seweryn Kowalski. She recited from memory the old translation by Father Jakub Wujek.[22] The whole community had several copies of the Old Testament for common use, edited by Father Stanisław Styś, SJ. The family gifted Sister Bernadette with her own copy of that edition a year before she died. It became for her "the summit of dreams, and a great and precious joy."[23] She believed that each sister should have the whole Bible. Given the financial challenges of the monastery at that time it seemed to be an unrealistic dream, but after several editions of the Millennium Bible were published, it became a reality. Sister Bernadette's intuition proved to be correct.

She once exclaimed, "Scripture is an inexhaustible mine; I keep finding new things in it, more and more beautiful." She especially loved the Psalms. For some time, the novices would choose, each taking a turn, the biblical verse of the week. Bernadette chose *Gustate et videte quoniam suavis est Dominus*, "O taste, and see that the Lord is sweet" (Ps 33:9).

Out of the three theological virtues, faith, hope, and charity, the first stood out to her. For a rather long time, she kept a card in her breviary with the words of the prophet Hosea: *Sponsabo te mihi in fide*, "I will espouse thee to me in faith" (Hos 2:20). She was fascinated by the person and story of Abraham, the "father of all believers." Once, during a conversation about those who don't believe in the Real Presence in the Blessed Sacrament, she exclaimed, "If Abraham had had the Eucharist in the Old Testament, he would have adored it by falling on his face." She was fond of the examples of faith in the Letter to the Hebrews, from the righteous Abel to the harlot Rahab (cf. Heb 11:1–33). She often read the Epistle to the Romans about justification by faith (cf. Rom 4).

---

21   The Millennium Bible is the main Polish Bible translation, first published in 1965 for the millennium of the Christianization of Poland in 966.

22   The Jakub Wujek Bible was the main Polish Bible in use from 1599 until 1965, when the Millennium Bible was published. The translation, based on the Vulgate, was done by the Jesuit Jakub Wujek. This would make it comparable to the Douay-Rheims version for English-speaking Catholics.

23   Letter to Danuta Szczepańska, April 15, 1962.

[Handwritten marginal note, left margin:] Makes sense she would love the Psalms w/ her artistic mind + ♡

Sister Bernadette's inner life, however, was most influenced by the Gospel. She shared Saint Augustine's conviction about the special experience of Christ's presence when she was reading it. She used to say that she could not live without reading the Gospel. When looking through the Gospel with Sabina Czerniewska, Sister Bernadette wanted to share with Sabina everything that was her life. After many years, Sabina said that when she opened the New Testament, she could still feel that contagious fascination. Sister Bernadette also knew and valued various commentaries on Scripture, not so much strictly exegetical works, but publications using the work of biblical scholars to help the interior life.

In the monastery she deepened her knowledge of the *Rule* of Saint Benedict, as the nuns are required to read it daily. She also read commentaries on the *Rule* by Benedictine authors, especially Dom Columba Marmion, whom she admired greatly. She read other worthwhile books by prominent authors as well. For a time, she was passionate about the works of Charles de Foucauld.[24] She would call him her "star," along with "the moon," Our Lady, and "the sun," Christ. Two books played a significant role in Sister Bernadette's interior life: *Clarisse de Jérusalem*, about Sister Mary of the Trinity,[25] and *He and I* by Gabrielle Bossis.[26] God, after all, has the right to speak to man

24   Blessed Charles Eugène de Foucauld, Viscount of Foucauld (1858–1916), was an officer in the French cavalry, an explorer and geographer, and finally a Catholic priest and hermit in Algeria, who was killed in 1916 by tribal raiders; his death has been considered that of a martyr for the Faith. His writings and example inspired the founding of the Little Sisters of Jesus and Little Brothers of Jesus, among other groups. He was beatified in 2005.

25   Louisa Jaques (1901–1942) was born in Pretoria, Transvaal, to French-Swiss Protestant parents; her mother died while giving birth to her. Her father, who was a Protestant missionary, took her back to Switzerland with her two elder sisters, and there they were brought up by her aunt. In the midst of a terrible crisis of faith, she received a visit from an unidentified nun, which turned her mind to thoughts of religious life. She eventually became Catholic, then entered religion as a Poor Clare, and at that point began being guided by an "inner voice," that of Our Lord, who led her to intimate union with Himself. Her spiritual director told her to write everything down. This diary is the book to which Sister Bernadette is referring and which she often quotes. In English: *The Spiritual Legacy of Sister Mary of the Holy Trinity: Poor Clare of Jerusalem, 1901–1942*, ed. Silvere van den Broek O. F. M. (Rockford, IL: TAN Books, 2009). Originally published in Belgium in 1950.

26   Gabrielle Bossis (1874–1950) was a French laywoman, actress, and mystic, whose book *Lui et Moi* records her dialogues with Jesus. She heard this "inner voice" and wrote down the words from the year 1936 to shortly before her death in 1950.

in any way that He deems fitting. Sister Bernadette always had the
Bible with her and almost always had her notes from the two books
mentioned above. They became part of the deposit of her inner life.

Christ remained at the center of Sister Bernadette's life, just as
He was for her great monastic founder, Saint Benedict. Her Chris-
tocentrism came to its fullness at the end of her life, at the offering
of the sacrifice.

She surrounded the entire life of Jesus Christ with love. She said
that once she was in heaven, she would demand to see a movie of
His life. Above all, she lived in the mystery of the Passion of Christ
and the sacrifice of the Cross. Before the Consecration of Virgins,
she wrote down texts from Isaiah about the suffering servant. One
of the cards that survived from this period bears the words of Saint
Paul: "For whom he foreknew, he also predestinated to be made
conformable to the image of his Son" (Rom 8:29). She was particularly impressed by the work *A Doctor at Calvary: The Passion of
Our Lord Jesus Christ as Described by a Surgeon*[27] written by Pierre
Barbet, a physician who recreated the Passion of Christ using the
Shroud of Turin. She venerated the Holy Face from the Shroud, and
spent hours contemplating both the face and the outline of the whole
body. "It gives me so much," she would say. She prepared for the
Consecration as if it were bloody nuptials, giving the logical reason,
"The nuptials with the Crucified One cannot be any other way." She
shocked the Prioress with the design of the cards for the ceremony.
Several red stains artfully splashed over white cardboard perfectly
imitated blood drops. Sister Bernadette signed this composition with
words taken from the Office of Saint Agnes, which was used in the
Rite of the Consecration of Virgins: *Immensis monilibus coronavit me*
(He hath adorned me with innumerable jewels). Mother Celestyna
had no reservations about the artistic vision and significance of the
card, but she suggested that Sister Bernadette paint something more
joyful, fearing that the nuns' families would not understand it. Thus,
Sister Bernadette left only two draft cards for Mother Celestyna
and Father Piotr, which unfortunately were later lost, and went on
to create "something more joyful." The final image was a cross with
an inscription woven into it, *Sponsus sanguinis tu mihi es*, "a bloody

---

27   This book was republished by Angelico Press in 2021.

SPONSUS
ANGUINIS
U MIHI ES
EXOD. 4. 25.

The commemorative card Sister Bernadette designed
for the Consecration of Virgins.

spouse art thou to me" (Ex 4:25), adorned with a branch of thorns.
"There was no choice, I had to make room for for the Passion of the
Cross and the shedding of blood." All the sisters liked this picture
very much.[28]

Sister Bernadette's nuptial relationship with Christ was tight-
ening over time. It was more and more an aware participation in
the exclusive love of Christ and the Church. Sister Bernadette was
passionate about the question of the "royal priesthood" (cf. 1 Pt 2:9),
and the Holy Spirit led her in this direction.

Her devotion to Our Lady was somewhat different. In the postulancy she cried because of her lack of feelings towards Our Lady.
She calmed down only when she realized that she was learning
humility by having to suffer this temporary defect. Gradually she
established a personal relationship with Mary. Saint Bernadette
Soubirous, enchanted by the beautiful Lady of the Massabielle grotto,
undoubtedly played a major role in this development. When one of

28 *Journals of Mother Celestyna Wielowieyska.*

the sisters was going through a hard time, Sister Bernadette left a holy card of those apparitions in her cell.

The image of Our Lady of Częstochowa was truly beloved to Sister Bernadette, but without the crowns and the elaborate dresses. She called Her "the most beautiful Mother of God in the world." She painted several good copies of the icon of the Black Madonna, adding to them, in a circle around the image, words in Latin taken from the Book of Wisdom and frequently read in the traditional missal, "For she is the brightness of eternal light, and the unspotted mirror of God's majesty, and the image of his goodness" (Wis 7:26). She also painted Our Lady as the Supreme Abbess of the Benedictine Nuns of Perpetual Adoration of the Blessed Sacrament, wearing a Benedictine cuculla, with a crosier in one hand and the Host in the other, surrounded by lilies that were bowing to her.[29]

Sister Bernadette's depiction of Saint Peter walking on the water.

29   For the houses of the Benedictines of Perpetual Adoration, Mother Mectilde decreed that the Blessed Virgin Mary be acknowledged as perpetual Abbess. This tradition probably came to Mother Mectilde by way of the Maurist Benedictine monks, who inherited it from the customs of Cluny. The invocation of Mary as Abbess in the monastic context is also present in the east, and she has been venerated under that title on Mount Athos for centuries.

*Sister Bernadette's image of Our Lady as Abbess with the
inscription, "Our Supreme Abbess, pray for us."*

EVANGELIARIUM

MONASTICUM

PRO FESTIS SUMMIS

IN FESTO
NATIVITATIS D.N.J.C

ORATIO

Concéde, quǽsumus, omnípotens Deus: ut nos
Unigéniti tui nova per carnem Nativitas lí-
beret, quos sub peccáti jugo vetústa sérvitus
tenet. Per eumdem Dóminum nostrum...

IN FESTO CORPORIS CHRISTI

ORATIO.

Deus, qui nobis sub Sacraménto mirábili passiónis tuae memóriam reliquísti: tríbue, quaésumus, ita nos Córporis et Sánguinis tui sacra mystéria venerári, ut redemptiónis tuae fructum in nobis júgiter sentiámus. Qui vivis.

IN FESTO PENTECOSTES

ORATIO

Deus, qui hodiérna die corda fidélium Sancti Spíritus illustratióne docuísti: da nobis in eódem Spíritu recta sápere; et de ejus semper consolatióne gaudére. Per Dóminum... in unitate ejusdem Spíritus Sancti.

Sister Bernadette made a Gospel book (Evangeliarium) to be used for high feasts at Matins, when the Collect and Gospel of the day are chanted by the officiant.

PRIE ELEISON

MÓJ BOŻE,myślę,że to
Ty do mnie mówisz.Wierzę,że moja
dusza w stanie łaski jest świątynią
gdzie realnie przebywa Bóg troiście
i jedynie święty,Bóg w Trzech Oso-
bach.W Tobie i przez Ciebie posiadam
tego Boga,posiadam te trzy Osoby.One kontynuują
we mnie życie wieczne,które jest ich wzajemną
i nieskończoną miłością ; One udzielają mi tego
życia,włączają mnie do wielkiej wymiany ich jedynego
bytu,gdzie Ojciec przelewa się zupełnie i cały
w Syna i gdzie Syn czyni to samo ;Oni żyją we mnie
tym tajemniczym darem i pełnią ich bytu,którym
jest ich wspólny Duch,ich miłość.Oni mnie zapraszają i dają się mi ,Jak oni się dają sobie wzajemn:
ną i zapraszają mnie do czynienia tego.

I Ty przybywasz na ziemię do pokazania nam
boskiego sekretu.Pozostajesz tu,obecny w taberna-
kulum,ofiarowujesz siebie na ołtarzu,dajesz się
w komunii i przez nią pokazujesz nam jak Bóg się

ój Boże,nie pójdę dziś
do Twojego domu ze ska-
ły;jestem unieruchomiony
w moim i wielki jest dy_
stans,który nas dzieli."

"Twoim prawdziwym domem jest nasza dusza i nasza miłość:"Jeśli ktoś mnie kocha,powiedziałeś,
zachowuje moje przykazania i my przyjdziemy
i zamieszkamy w nim."/Jan XIV,23/.Moja dusza
jest więc sanktuarium,gdzie Ty przebywasz.

Mogę łączyć się z Tobą,adorować Ciebie,kochać
i rozmawiać z Tobą; przedstawiać Ci swoje potrze-
by,omyłki i także,dlaczego nie,swoje postępy
i wysiłki.Mogę powierzać Ci moje małe zmartwie-
nia jednocząc je z twoimi tak wielkimi.Mogę ofiarować Tobie siebie,z wszystkim tym,co jest mója
istotą i życiem ,przez które Ty uczyń ze mną,
to co chcesz.Jestem tak pewny,że to,co Ty zrobisz
będzie moim największym dobrem i Twoją największą
chwałą. Mogę Cię prosić,byś mi dał siebie,udzielił

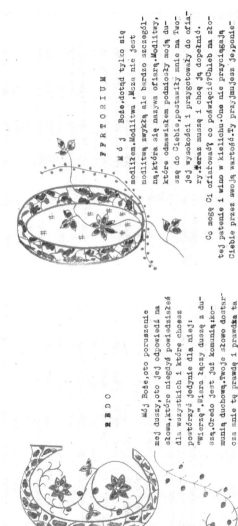

R B D O

Mój Boże,oto poruszenie
mej duszy,oto jej odpowiedź na
słowa,które niegdyś powiedziałeś
dla wszystkich i które chcesz
powtórzyć jedynie dla niej;
"Wierzę".Wiara łączy duszę z du-
szą.Credo jest już komunią,ko-
munią duchową.Twoje słowo dostar-
cza mnie tę prawdę i prawdła ta
jest Tobą."Ja jestem Prawdą"
(Jan XIV,6),powiedziałeś.I dodałeś"Ja jestem Drogą",
"Jam jest Życie" i "Ci,którzy wierzą we mnie otrzy-
mają życie wieczne!"

To jest prawda,życie jest wewnętrzną relac-
ją pomiędzy dwoma bytami,które pozwalają się prze-
lewać jednemu w drugie.Byt wyższy udziela drugiemu
życie wyższe.Kiedy ustawiam moje ciało w relacji

F F R T O R I U M

Mój Boże,dotąd tylko się
modlitem.Modlitwa ,Msza nie jest
modlitwą zwykłą ale bardzo szczególną,która się nazywa ofiarą.Modlitwy,
które odnawiałem podniosły moją duszę do Ciebie,postawiły mnie na Twojej wysokości i przygotowały do ofia-
ry.Teraz muszę i chcę ją dopełnić.

Co mogę Ci ofiarować? co poświęcić?Chleb na zło-
tej patenie i wino w kielichu.One nie przyciągają
Ciebie przez swoje wartość.Ty przyjmujesz je,ponie-
waż one mają stać się Twoim Ciałem I Krwią,i że pod
tą formą możesz dać dostęp Twoim pragnieniom poch-
łaniającym Cię,by się związać z nami abyśmy się
przemienili w Ciebie.

Przemiana w Ciebie,łączność z Tobą samym,
nieskończoną i wieczną pięknem,biedni,ubodzy i tak
pełni słabości i nędzy;jedność czyli wspólność myśli,
uczuć,pragnień,działania.oto Twoje miłosne i boskie
marzenia.Chleb i wino,którymi chcesz nas nakarmić :

Pages illuminated by Sister Bernadette from a typescript of The Mass of a Soul, *written by an anonymous Carthusian monk.*

This small drawing connects the Sursum Corda of the Mass with Christ's ascension. "I can clearly see that this new life broadened her heart," Mrs. Wolska said of her daughter.

Sister Bernadette "of the Cross" was no stranger to that mystery. Here are two versions of a design with words from Saint John, "We have believed the charity" (1 Jn 4:16). Love hangs on the cross, as does the "C" of caritati.

Humility, sin, and suffering

After Sister Bernadette's death, Father Piotr Rostworowski wrote to her mother, "She possessed one of the rarest virtues: humility."[30] Mother Celestyna, who knew her equally well regarding her interior life, confirmed this judgment: "The grace of self-denial of which she dreamed in the novitiate ... was granted to her abundantly."[31] All those who knew Sister Bernadette can verify these testimonies. The community cherished the memory of her preparing for confession with tears and apologizing to them before her Solemn Profession. During the chapter of faults, when the nuns confess their external faults committed against the community and its discipline, Sister Bernadette's self-accusations were so strong and blunt that the sisters often asked the Prioress not to allow her to make those confessions. Mother Celestyna, however, could not grant these requests: "I felt ... that by such a prohibition I would have caused her grief and would only have embarrassed her — so sincere and spontaneous were those confessions of her heart, full of self-disregard and self-contempt."[32]

Sister Bernadette had an exceptionally clear awareness of the gravity of sin. In an age of relativism and of diminished human responsibility, her attitude stands out as a sign and a warning. She had the courage to acknowledge the dark reality of her own guilt and to emulate David's attitude towards it: "My sin is always before me" (Ps 50:5). She called the evil she committed "boorishness" towards God. This was a manifestation of her greatness. The God of "the humble and the meek" is also "the God of all power and might" (cf. Jdt 9:11, 14). He gives the strength to accomplish the greatest victory in a person's life — the eradication of one's own selfishness. Sister Bernadette knew that this was possible only through relying on Christ's humility. She wrote, "Let us pray ... for this joyful and victorious self-denial."[33]

In this veneration of humility, which is the recognition of the truth about oneself and the world, lie the roots of Sister Bernadette's veneration of reality: first of the great Reality of God, and then of

---

30   Letter of May 5, 1963.
31   *Journals of Mother Celestyna Wielowieyska.*
32   Ibid.
33   Letter to her mother, January 31, 1963.

the small everyday reality. One of her note cards read, "Remembering that which IS — that is why God graciously tears down our plans, built on nothingness, so that we may anchor ourselves in Him."[34] Her favorite sentence from the book *Clarisse de Jérusalem* became the succinct, "It is enough to be."

It was not in vain that Sister Bernadette was "of the Cross." It accompanied her always. While the difficulties related to her painting talent diminished with time, her physical ailments intensified. The surgery in 1955 did not help much. Although she dreamed of exercising strict observance, she had to avail herself of dispensations and follow a special diet throughout her life.

She was not like those sick people who constantly complain. When writing to her family, especially to her mother, she tried to downplay her ailments. She was not demanding. Recognizing the extreme poverty of the monastery, she never demanded expensive medicine. She never avoided work under the pretext of being unwell but worked to the point of exhaustion. When one of the sisters was surprised that Sister Bernadette, the day before she went to the hospital, was still attending to matters related to her monastery office, she replied, "Sister, do you know what responsibility is?"

At the same time, she had a lot of medical ideas and liked to diagnose herself and propose certain treatments. This sometimes tired the infirmary sisters and did not always prove the most successful in fighting the disease itself. It was a certain natural personality flaw, which with a less intense inner life could have developed into hypochondria. However, Sister Bernadette was not excessively concerned with herself and her health. She remained open to God's reality and the needs of her neighbor.

Chastity, poverty, obedience

Life itself provided her with opportunities for sacrifice. It has been rightly said of religious vows that they are the three nails that fasten man to the Cross.

Already during her Tyniec years, one of the oblates noticed Rozmarynka's striking restraint, which she seemed to have placed as the guard of her virginity. She was neither prudish nor vulgar. "I think

---

34   From the monastery archive.

she reached the simplicity and innocence of a child," wrote another
sister. However, a vow is not made for nothing. Although there was
something boyish in Sister Bernadette's appearance and manner, at the
same time she did not lack femininity and a maternal disposition. She
simply adored children. Pictures of her nephews and nieces adorned
her cell and took the place of holy cards in her breviary. This proved
that by renouncing physical motherhood she made a great sacrifice,
which urged her to live spiritual motherhood even more deeply.

Sister Bernadette unreservedly accepted the considerable penury
of the religious house and the prevalent manner of observing poverty.
For a long time, for lack of a proper table, she painted posters while
kneeling on the floor. She repaired personal belongings until they
completely fell apart, which made her wear, according to her mother,
"holes and patches truly modeled after Saint Francis."[35] Sometimes
it was even entertaining. Once, she mended her black habit with a
large navy blue patch, which made all the sisters laugh. Then she
painted the patch black. Some forms of poverty practiced by Sister
Bernadette are no longer relevant today. These days, when synthetic
fibers have replaced cotton and wool, it doesn't make sense to repair
clothes with holes. Nevertheless, the way in which Sister Bernadette
practiced poverty also contains values that are still relevant today.
She took care to be authentic in her poverty. She was careful not
to have too many personal items. On one occasion, a sister told
Sister Bernadette that she liked to remove superfluous items from
her cell so as not to leave a mess after her death. Sister Bernadette
got excited, "You know what? So do I."

She was very meticulous about the most precious temporal good
of modern man: time. "Time does not belong to me anymore," she
wrote and repeated many times. She brought her work even to the
parlor, and often gave it to her guests.

Was poverty hard for her? She was an artist, and an independent
soul in a way. She accepted without resistance those forms of "strict"
poverty which brought her closer to original simplicity. At the same
time, it overwhelmed her with an excessive amount of exhausting
work, which, as mentioned earlier, was mostly not to her liking. In
that way it became the nail of her crucifixion.

---

35 *Mother's Journal*, part 1, p. 38.

The greatest sacrifice for her, however, was surrendering her will. As a choleric, Sister Bernadette was the dictatorial, independent type. In choosing the religious life, she made a choice of total self-denial.

Obedience to the chosen, beloved, but not at all easy *Rule* cost her dearly. Obedience to the Novice Mistress and then the Prioress, Mother Celestyna Wielowieyska, also cost her. Mother Celestyna distinguished herself by leading renovation works on the monastery. A woman of exceptional manners, she devoted herself fully to the community and loved every sister like a mother. However, she was not an easy superior. Blessed with exceptional mystical graces, she sometimes set the bar too high, and others did not always live up to her standards. Like every human being, she made mistakes. Both the superior and the subordinate were strong personalities, which frequently led to conflicts between them. However, Sister Bernadette always returned to Mother Celestyna with humility and contrition. "She always spoke of Mother Prioress with the greatest love."[36]

Sisters bring to the order's community life their good will, but also their human qualities, including weaknesses. Even flaws, as in the case of Sister Bernadette, can become the raw material of holiness. The religious community, which is the Church in miniature, has its specific charism, and tensions and disagreements between sisters are dissolved in God's peace.

Goal for family life, too

Amidst the community ✱ *Great connections b/t monastic life + family life*

Sister Bernadette had a great love for her community and was one of its most beloved members. She was one of their own, which, as one sister expressed it, "meant that she was imbued with the spirit of the order, devoted to the monastery, and the monastery could certainly rely on her." All that could be said, even though she never held any important positions in religious life due to the volume of her work as a painter. For a time, she was the assistant cantor, the assistant mistress of ceremonies, and in later years a councillor.[37] However, she

---

36   *Mother's Journal*, part 2, p. 4.

37   In a monastic context, a councillor refers to a religious chosen by the Superior or voted by the rest of the community to be one of the members of the Superior's private council. In addition to having a consultatory role for the Superior, the council also has various functions according to Canon Law whereby their consent, indicated by voting, is required for certain important

participated fully in the life of the community and shared its fortunes.

Sister Bernadette tried her hardest to implement in her life a phrase of Mother Mectilde of the Blessed Sacrament that particularly struck her: "We are to have a special love for those who inflict suffering on us, for they are the priests who offer us up to God."

Despite the initial, understandable reaction, she did not bear any grudges after being hurt, and she accepted with joy even undeserved admonitions. She was not a helpless and vulnerable person by nature. She had a tough, impulsive character. Although she kept herself in check, sometimes things got out of hand. However, when tensions arose, she did not ask, "Who started it? Who was more at fault?" Sometimes, objectively speaking, the fault was more someone else's, at other times it was more hers. In both cases, she was the first to humbly seek reconciliation.

It so happened that she had an argument with one of the sisters. It was exactly at the time that she was moving to the first single cell in her religious life. That sister, wanting to make up for her misconduct, decided to scrub the new cell in complete secrecy. However, it so happened that Sister Bernadette walked in on her performing the task. They threw themselves into each other's arms, crying with emotion over their reconciliation.

Another time it involved a minor wrong done to one of the sisters, which hardly affected her. After Sister Bernadette had made amends to her for this shortcoming, the "wronged" sister spoke to her about the true worth that may be hidden in our failures. Sister Bernadette nodded, and her eyes showed visible regret that she had grieved the Lord and her neighbor. "Then I felt even more love and respect for her," wrote the other sister.

Sister Bernadette, an astute observer, easily noticed the weaknesses of those around her. She carefully avoided detraction and her motto was, "Guard your tongue." Occasionally it did happen that she judged someone too hastily, but she immediately checked herself. Her former Novice Mistress wrote, "I can clearly see her childlike fearful glance and this readiness to compensate, to do everything, to trample herself, as long as she could be reconciled with God, as long as she could look at Him calmly." She never returned to a matter once closed. She

---

community matters, such as the expenditure of funds over a certain amount.

often repeated, especially to sisters prone to scruples, "Don't give it another thought, there is no need to split hairs." She was equally careful about the righteousness of her thoughts and intentions. She wrote down the following notable sentence from the work *Clarisse de Jérusalem*:

> The greatest love you can have for each other does not consist in making gifts to each other or in performing services; it is in your thoughts.... The sisters must find in you a kind thought that understands and comprehends them.

In community life, Sister Bernadette also won over hearts with gratitude. The sister in charge of clothing and linen said that mending her things was a true pleasure. Likewise, the sister who handled her shopping received an enthusiastic note after buying each item: "Thank you most sincerely, everything was wonderfully done!"

The community was struck by Sister Bernadette's genuine humility. She could contribute a lot to joint meetings and recreation. She was intelligent, witty, well-read, and familiar with the world. Her words provided much food for thought. However, she never grew too chatty. She carefully avoided taking the spotlight. It was also in *Clarisse de Jérusalem* that she found the phrase: "To be — and not to show oneself off." Although she did not give up the gift of spiritual friendship in the monastery, at recreation she tended to sit next to the sisters who were lonely that day, who were going through some difficulty, or who had recently gone from the novitiate to the community of professed sisters. Her listening attentively to others, sometimes a seemingly insignificant word, giving up a better seat to someone — all that brought her closer to God and strengthened the unity of the community. Sister Bernadette's common sense was the reason she never gave up her sharp and blunt humor. Sometimes words were replaced by her laughter or a smile, with a sparkle of mischief in her eyes.

As time went on, she blended more and more into the background of the community. Initially setting the tone during singing lessons, she later refrained from commenting, adapting to those sisters who were less musically gifted. She served with her talent, above all and beyond measure. Despite being constantly overworked, she found the time to do some drawing and painting for sisters who had asked her. When asked who she kept painting for (it was an open secret), she would only answer with a roguish smile. Sometimes she anticipated requests. Handing over a picture that she knew was the dream of one of the Benedictine nuns, she said to her with joy, "I thought of you sister, I wanted to give this to you." She often gave sisters pictures painted for them for their religious celebrations. She also wrote down homilies delivered on such occasions (the monastery did not acquire a tape recorder until 1961).

Sister Bernadette filled in for others at the gatehouse and in Adoration, and also made herself available to help during feast days. She used to dress up the "actresses" who performed in the monastery plays and made wonderful animal masks of a cat or a lion. Although she did not enjoy those activities very much, she did not shirk from participating in them. Her voice was recorded on tape in two parts: that of an old woman and that of a reporter in the nuns' radio broadcast *Le Dieu Vivant* (*The Living God*) by Cita and Suzanne Malard.[38]

Especially at the end of her days, Sister Bernadette was sensitive to the perfection of the commandment that Jesus called His own (cf. Jn 15:12) and the litmus test of Christian authenticity: "By this shall all men know that you are my disciples, if you have love one for another" (Jn 13:35). She offered help to whomever she could. "How good it is that before we die, we can still do something good," she once said, with a telling look. She performed these good deeds in secret, as Christ taught (cf. Mt 6:4); she did not want them to be known, nor did she want to be thanked for them, which actually caused her distress.

An apostolate from within

Her love did not end at the monastery walls. For Sister Bernadette, as for the whole monastic tradition, the contemplative life was at the same time the apostolic life (*vita apostolica*), giving to others from superabundance, first through prayer, and then also through active help.

---

38   For more information, see https://journals.openedition.org/skenegraphie /1227.

Above all, Sister Bernadette was concerned with the problems of the Church, both eternal and temporal. She was very interested in the works of Pius XII, his Eucharistic and liturgical reforms, and the Marian Year proclaimed by him in 1954. She had a special reverence and affection for his successor, John XXIII.

She was moved to prayer by the notice of the convocation of an Ecumenical Council on January 25, 1959. She wrote a letter to one of the Council commissions arguing that the People of God should have the right to speak to the Heavenly Father in their native language during the liturgy. At the time, the issue stirred up much controversy. Sister Bernadette lived to see the opening of the first session of the Second Vatican Council on October 11, 1962, and she closely followed the discussion on the liturgy (a report on the Council's deliberations was read daily in the refectory), which had already resolved to introduce vernacular languages into the celebrations.[39] However, she did not live to see these resolutions approved.

Sister Bernadette was entrusted with an undeniably prestigious task. She made the album of the Council, which the Primate, Stefan Cardinal Wyszyński,[40] presented as a gift from Poland to John

---

39   The debates in the first session of the Council involved a consistent emphasis on the retention of Latin as a liturgical language, alongside a more extended (but not exclusive) use of the vernacular. This balanced position found its way into the Constitution on the Sacred Liturgy, *Sacrosanctum concilium*: see nn. 36, 54, 91, 101, and 116.

40   Blessed Stefan Wyszyński (1901–1981) was born in the village of Zuzela in eastern Mazovia, which at that time was part of the Russian Empire. Ordained on his twenty-third birthday, after finishing his studies he taught at the seminary in Włocławek. When World War II broke out he was forced to leave on account of friction with the Nazis, and went to Laski near Warsaw. He aided escaping Jews and, during the Warsaw Uprising, he assumed the pseudonym "Radwan II" and worked as a chaplain in the resistance. Shortly after the war, Wyszyński was appointed Bishop of Lublin (1946–1948), and then Archbishop of Warsaw and Archbishop of Gniezno from 1948 to 1981. He was created a Cardinal on January 12, 1953, by Pope Pius XII. Tensions between the postwar Stalinist government and the Church were extremely severe and although Wyszyński was able to negotiate over the issue of state seizure of ecclesiastical property, a new persecution broke out in 1953, just following his elevation to the Cardinalate. Wyszyński and numerous other priests were imprisoned. Released in 1956, his efforts for the furthering of the Catholic faith were highlighted in the 1966 celebration of Poland's Millennium of Christianity, although the Communist authorities refused to allow Pope Paul VI to visit. Pope John Paul II's 1979

XXIII. While performing this task she incurred, in her own opinion, great culpability. Someone advised her to sign the album, and so she did. Later she sincerely regretted that she had stepped out of the shadows and ceased to be hidden.

As for the Council, she primarily prayed for its deliberations. She said she was constantly "bugging God for its intentions." During the first session she is remembered to have written on the bulletin board that we should pray "for our dear Bishops." She commended the Council to God on the day of her death.

Her apostolate embraced various groups of people, the first of which was her family. Writing in her diary shortly after her daughter's death, Mrs. Wolska stated that Sister Bernadette's interest in family matters did not diminish over the years, but increased: "I can clearly see that this new life broadened her heart."[41] She was especially concerned about the still unresolved matter of her father's second relationship, which reached an unexpected conclusion. When, due to his advanced age, Kazimierz Wolski required assistance, he was sent back to his wife in 1962. Mrs. Wolska behaved heroically and accepted him without a word of reproach. Sister Bernadette also expressed her joy at the admittedly involuntary but real return of her father. During Advent of 1962 her parents spent two days at the monastery. That was the last time that Sister Bernadette saw her father. That meeting was overshadowed by the awareness that he had not been reconciled with God. This did not happen until after her death. Kazimierz Wolski died four years after his daughter, and his wife outlived him by seven years. After a difficult life, she had a beautiful death. She died on June 5, 1974, immediately after receiving Holy Communion.

Sister Bernadette's direct apostolate spread widely. She was often visited by her cousins, friends, and acquaintances from her secular life. Some meetings were truly providential and had a great influence on the lives of many people. Among them was a senior official of the French embassy, who was simply enchanted by the Polish nun.

---

visit to Poland was the triumphant culmination of the two prelates' years of collaboration for the survival of the Catholic Faith in Poland. Wyszyński died less than a month after the May 13, 1981 assassination attempt on the Pope, offering his life for the Holy Father. Stefan Wyszyński's cause for canonization was introduced in 1989, and he was beatified on September 12, 2021.

41 *Mother's Journal*, part 1, p. 36.

Sister Bernadette exerted her influence with her entire persona. Her common sense, childlike simplicity, maturity, and godly charm, that is, sincerity, appealed to others more than any theoretical considerations. A candidate who was doing a two-week retreat at the monastery was especially captivated by her genuineness and commitment to religious life. It helped her realize the value of living a contemplative life and she entered the monastery. Sister Bernadette later surrounded this vocation with prayer and discreet solicitude.

She was also an apostle of joy. When Mrs. Wolska's brother, Andrzej Sozański, who lived permanently in Canada, visited Poland, their ample afternoon tea was filled with laughter from both sides of the cloister grille. "My brother left amused and charmed by his cloistered niece . . . . He had not anticipated such an experience in the cloister."[42]

She sometimes became involved in the active apostolate. During these years she met again with Sabina Czerniawska. She considered the possibility that her guest might have a vocation to the cloister, but then decided that she was more suited to the Congregation of Franciscan Sisters Servants of the Cross in Laski.[43] There was even talk in the monastery that if there was still such a thing as the Confraternity of the Blessed Sacrament, which used to exist, Sister Bernadette would have made a perfect promoter for it.

A retreat for eternity

Two years before her death, however, Sister Bernadette realized that God wanted her to renounce these relationships. She presented the problem to her superior and to her confessor, who accepted her decision. From that time on she went to see her guests only to apologize to them that she could not spend more than five minutes with them. These two years of almost complete lack of contact with the world were like a retreat that prepared her for eternity.

As long as we live in the world, we are merely pilgrims, *viatores*. The fullness intended by God is reached at the stroke of the right

---

42   *Mother's Journal,* part I, p. 39.
43   The Congregation of Franciscan Sisters Servants of the Cross was founded by Blessed Róża Czacka in 1918; their charism is serving the blind. They run a special school for blind and visually impaired children in Laski, just outside of Warsaw.

hour, as it was in the life of Christ. It was no different for Sister Bernadette. Thanks to that, her life is shown to us as an example to be imitated.

Even though she was a cloistered nun, she shared the fate of her contemporaries, and not only in the secular stage of her life, when she was a child sentenced to death before birth and then coming from a broken family, which forced her to earn a living prematurely. Within the cloister, daily hard work and exhaustion became her life. Living in a community, she had to surrender to its regulations and limit her freedom for the sake of the community. She suffered from diseases that were rampant at the time, possibly of psychogenic origin.

Sister Bernadette is worthy of emulation also because her life was not a perfect hagiographic story of a saint who seemed impeccable from the cradle to the grave. She was never proper or flawless. Was she a saint, then? The nuns, reluctant to recognize holiness too hastily, declared that she had left behind an example of humble holiness. Her relatives, too, were struck by her extraordinary transformation after only a few years of living in the monastery. "She was such an ordinary girl and yet she changed so much, became so mature," remembered Danuta Szczepańska. The monastery became for her a holy land, a place of covenant, a place of revelation of God in Jesus Christ. The story of her life was captured in her favorite passage from the Book of Hosea: "And I will espouse thee to me for ever: and I will espouse thee to me in justice, and judgment, and in mercy, and in commiserations. And I will espouse thee to me in faith: and thou shalt know that I am the Lord" (Hos 2:19–20).

"Cut me in strips, but let them return to You and give You glory."

3
Sacrifice and Death

Premonition of death

Sister Bernadette had a sense of the brevity of our earthly life: to use biblical language, a realization of the fact that "we all die, and like waters that return no more, we fall down into the earth" (2 Sm 14:14). When thanking her mother for the warm clothes she had sent her, she wrote, "Somehow I did not imagine that I would be living in the monastery for several years."[1] It is clear from her letters that she cherished each moment with the conviction that she would not be given many. Probably a year before her death, during recreation, she shared with one of the sisters her reflection on the reading from the Sunday before the Ascension, "We have heard of it in Ephrata.... Arise, O Lord, into thy resting place!" (Ps 131:6, 8). Sister commented, "Arise, Lord, you have already toiled enough."

The premonition of death took on a practical dimension. Sister Bernadette asked, for example, that her missing teeth not be replaced, because "What for? I may not need them anymore." She surprised everyone when she decided to iron her cuculla at recreation. Several months later, she would be wearing it in the coffin. She withdrew more and more from worldly matters, as they concerned her no more. At a meeting of the monastery council, she made a request to have more conversations about God at recreation, like the disciples of Emmaus, who talked about the Lord and their hearts were burning with His love (Lk 24:32). She could no longer speak without tears about God's goodness and her own wickedness.

A morbid predilection for death was completely foreign to her personality, bursting with life. One of the sisters once said that, like Saint Thérèse of Lisieux and Saint Elizabeth of the Trinity, she would like to die young. Sister Bernadette replied that she would gladly live even a hundred years, just to attain a slight growth in charity.

---

1 Letter to her mother, December 17, 1953.

However, she had the intuitive feeling that a long life would not be given to her. Even these almost thirty-six years of her life should be divided into two periods of almost identical length. The first period of Rozmarynka Wolska's life was spent, to use monastic terminology, *in regione dissimilitudinis*,[2] in the sphere of reality foreign to God. Her first "conversion" was the still vague awakening of religious interests in Wilków. Her next conversion was brought by the period of interaction with the oblates of Tyniec, her admission to the oblates, entering the monastery, and the subsequent stages of her religious initiation in the monastery. However, there was one moment which Sister Bernadette herself called the moment of conversion in the full sense of the word. In addition to a ten-day retreat, the Benedictine Nuns of Perpetual Adoration of the Blessed Sacrament participate in a three-day retreat at the beginning of each year, which starts with the renewal of their vows. In 1961, this three-day retreat was led by Father Aleksander Fedorowicz. The talks from this retreat were transcribed from a tape recording and, with slight abbreviations, they were published in one volume of a several-volume collection.[3] Those talks, so profound in their simplicity and straightforwardness, given by a man who had come close to death himself, had a shocking effect on Sister Bernadette. For the first time she was unable to write anything down. She decided to repent. This happened already a year after she had decided to limit her contacts with "the world" to a minimum.

Her health deteriorates

Sister Bernadette's desire to offer her life as a holocaust matured more and more. She regarded it as a normal culmination of the life of a Benedictine Nun of Perpetual Adoration, an oblation for Jesus Christ, an oblation for God the Father. Sister Bernadette did not think that the life of a Benedictine nun should be a chain of elaborate torments. She used to say that all she wanted was to be always on the lookout, close to God, with a knife to her throat so that He could strike the blow at any moment He chose. She used

---

2   "In the region of dissimilarity"—a phrase from Saint Augustine.

3   *W nurcie zagadnień soborowych* [Discussing Conciliar Questions], Fr. Aleksander Fedorowicz, *W Kościele dzisiejszym* [In Today's Church], (Warsaw, 1975), vol. 7.

to say, "Suffering is for love." She knew that it became meaningful only when it served the salvific work of Christ.

The direction of her sacrifice increasingly took on a priestly character. She wrote down the following sentence from *Clarisse de Jérusalem*: "Pray more for priests and co-workers." When conversing with a sister about what heaven would be like, she remarked, "I think about meeting Melchizedek." This king and priest who offered bread and wine, "likened unto the Son of God," prefigures the priesthood of Christ (cf. Gn 14:17–20; Heb 7:1–28).

What could have caused Sister Bernadette's death? There were lesions on her reproductive organs. General weakness, weight loss, fever, strong paroxysmal pains for some time pointed to tuberculosis in those organs. Just before going to the hospital she confessed that every step, every word, and every movement were difficult for her. During the last year of her life, she was granted extensive dispensations; she did not attend the Divine Office, and only occasionally came to community recreation. She was exempt from household chores, which are shared by all nuns by virtue of belonging to the community. Sister Bernadette did not treat this period as a time of rest. She voluntarily burdened herself with so many additional tasks that her life did not become any easier. Objectively speaking, however, her illness was not incurable. The tests conducted in the hospital ruled out tuberculosis. The tumor turned out to be benign, and only its location and inflammation caused the alarming symptoms. Modern medicine can handle similar cases perfectly well. However, that is not what happened here. Firstly, the choice of the clinic played a big role. Mother Celestyna wanted to send her to Transfiguration Hospital, where the monastery could count on friendly medical and nursing care. It is within the superior's jurisdiction to make such decisions, but she would usually defer to the opinion of the ill sister. The doctor who took care of Sister Bernadette referred her to another hospital, to be treated by the supposedly excellent specialists. Based on that, Sister Bernadette took this referral as God's will. Mother Celestyna, although clearly apprehensive, chose to respect that view.

Although in her letters Sister Bernadette tried to downplay her ailments, they caused her great pain. She treated her illness and the endless unpleasant examinations and treatments, during which she would often shed tears (she would say, "The tears are coming on their own"), as a way of reparation to God for sins of profanation of the body and spreading moral corruption. Like Christ, stripped of his garments, she had to allow herself to be "stripped to the point of nakedness" (*Clarisse de Jérusalem*) because this is the condition and destiny of a sacrificial victim. She consciously accepted this sacrifice.

She was scheduled to go to the hospital on March 1, 1963. In her typical manner, Sister Bernadette made fun of herself even at that moment. Generally, however, her farewell with the sisters was serious and emotional. "Who knows if I will come back?," she said to one of them. She apologized for all the wrongs she had done and asked for prayers during her life and after her death so that she would not remain in purgatory for long. This premonition of her imminent death was shared by some of the sisters.

Wishing not to alarm her parents, especially her mother, Sister Bernadette decided not to notify them at all about her illness. The only family member who knew was Danuta Szczepańska. However, Mrs. Wolska found out about the hospital stay a month later, although not directly from her daughter.

But let them return to you

The first month was spent on tests and treatments, including the treatment of the inflammation. Sister Bernadette wrote, "I am not bored for a moment because I have things to read and to do. Besides, lying down is also a pleasant activity when you feel poorly."[4] Again, in her typical way, she used the stay in the hospital as an opportunity for her apostolate. It was during conversations with other patients that her fate was determined, before the doctors decided anything.

At that time, news spread about certain actions of one of the so-called Patriot Priests[5] who served the Communist Regime which

---

4   Letter to N. N., March 6, 1963.
5   A noteworthy feature of Communism's anti-religious campaigns in Poland during these years was the rewarding of priests who expressed communist sympathies in opposition to the Church hierarchy. Bolesław Bierut (1892–1956), the first postwar president of Poland and leading supporter of Stalinist and Socialist ideologies in Poland, blamed the Catholic hierarchy's anti-communist stance for making the clergy express views which were "criminal", and gave priests who collaborated with the state privileges which included financial

was hostile towards the Church. The matter was also discussed with much pain in the monastery. A tendentious propaganda book he had published, which described moral scandals reputedly committed by priests, monks, and nuns, reached the patients of the gynecological ward in the hospital where Sister Bernadette was being treated. She was told about dreadful "facts" taken from the book. Listening to those horrors was very painful to her. The story of a priest who betrayed and trampled the priesthood of Christ made her remember other painful facts from priests' lives which were known to her: the stories of those who had abandoned or betrayed their priesthood. She had the impression that a bucket of excrement had been poured over her. She felt incredible pain, both spiritual and physical, as if Christ himself were suffering in her. In an act of voluntary sacrifice, she said to Him, "Cut me in strips, but let them return to You and give You glory." She realized that her sacrifice was accepted and she was filled with a solemn peace.

The surgery was scheduled for Thursday, April 4, 1963. Sister Kinga was granted leave from the cloister to attend to her in the most difficult time after the surgery. When she arrived in the morning, Sister Bernadette was sitting on the bed and her teeth were chattering. When asked if she had chills, she replied, "No, it's just like that." She was filled with anxiety before the surgery but tried to control it. She was given an injection and taken to the operating room. Despite her previous requests, she was not operated on by the chief surgeon, but by a young doctor whose name was never revealed to the monastery. The surgery lasted over two hours. The uterus and some of the other organs were removed. At the same time the purulent appendix was also removed.

At this point, her prognosis was excellent. Sister Bernadette suffered a lot, was unable to sleep, and she relieved her thirst by sucking on wet gauze, but that is normal after surgery. Her body temperature remained normal for her condition (99–100 degrees Fahrenheit), her pulse steady and strong. She was given IV fluids and lay quietly, occasionally asking for something. The next night a hired nurse kept watch over her. Sister Kinga continued to visit her until Palm Sunday,

support, vacations, and tax-exemption. Needless to say, the so-called "Patriot Priests" received little support from the Catholic laity.

when, to Sister Bernadette's great joy, she brought blessed palms. Sister Bernadette dictated to her a letter to Father Piotr. She wrote that she felt like an astronaut sent into space whose spaceship was steered by God Himself, and that now she was viewing the world in a completely different way. She loyally admitted that not everyone would agree to pay such a high price of suffering for this experience. Despite the seriousness of her thoughts, the letter was "playful," as Father Piotr described it. Father did not have the time to write back. He did not learn of Sister Bernadette's serious condition until shortly before her death, when he was unable to come.

Meanwhile, the patient was beginning to get up and walk around the hospital room. It was obvious that she was plagued by hunger, because she would often talk about food. When smelling oranges, she said with a roguish smile that the days of binge eating would fall during the Easter Triduum. Although things were going well for the time being, she would confess that she longed to die in order to be finally reunited with God. She said, however, that she couldn't play a prank on her mother, because it was only fitting that one's mother should get to heaven first.

Complications

The first complications occurred on Tuesday, April 9: gastrointestinal issues. For the time being they were relatively mild, and the doctor did not seem concerned about them. On Holy Thursday, April 11, Sister Bernadette painted a picture of the Lamb for one of the other patients and two Easter cards.

Her condition remained stable until Holy Saturday. Then the first symptoms of intestinal obstruction developed, which were ignored. During the Easter Vigil and Easter Sunday Mass, Sister Bernadette was writhing in pain. Meanwhile, the radio in the room was playing secular songs.

She suffered terribly over the next four days, although the pains came with varying intensity and were of different duration. It was later discovered that the pain was caused by a twisted bowel and intestinal adhesions. A sense of inner sadness, hopelessness, and abandonment by God aggravated the distress. Even Christ did not escape a struggle with it. For Sister Bernadette it was a condition of becoming like the Lord. The cup of His Passion is to be drunk to the lees.

On Easter Sunday, Sister Bernadette informed the monastery by telephone that she was feeling much worse. Sister Kinga rushed to her immediately and was horrified at the state in which she found her, since the illness caused such devastation. The doctors continued to see nothing alarming in these symptoms. One of the specialists claimed that it was spastic colon, another that it was a regular digestive disorder, a third suspected a duodenal ulcer. In the end, they unanimously decided that these internal problems were not their responsibility and declared the sister's dismal condition to be normal after surgery.

All she got was a 250 ml glucose drip with Cebion.[6] Nothing more was given, despite her requests.

On Tuesday, April 15, the eve of her religious name day, in the absence of Sister Kinga, she asked for a priest with the holy oils. The power of the Sacrament of Extreme Unction turned out to be of utmost necessity during the terrible night from Tuesday to Wednesday. The sufferings were constantly increasing. The nurse on duty agreed with Sister Kinga that Sister Bernadette had been left with no doctor caring for her, but she felt helpless in the face of their indifference.

The situation deteriorated even further by the time Mrs. Wolska had arrived in Warsaw on Easter Tuesday. She wanted to hug her daughter before her return to the cloister and to help her with the return to the monastery. She visited her on Wednesday morning. Their greeting was heartrending: "Mama, don't resent me for trying to get to heaven before you." When asked what bothered her most, she replied that it was feebleness — "so deep, to the very bottom of the Valley of Jehoshaphat."[7]

Those few days of neglect determined Sister Bernadette's fate. In that particular case it served God's purpose, but it can be a warning for doctors who limit themselves only to their narrow specializations. Neither the head physician, who was on leave at that time and came to the hospital only occasionally, nor his deputy wanted to give a diagnosis and referral to another clinic. Those taking care of the sister tried to transfer her on their own, but it was very hard to do that.

---

6   A medicine in drops containing vitamin C to strengthen immunity.

7   C.f. Joel 3:2–14, where the prophet announces that when the Lord restores Judah and Jerusalem, he will gather all the nations in the Valley of Jehoshaphat for an apocalyptic judgment.

Urged by the requests, the deputy physician finally issued a referral on Wednesday, April 16. Sisters Kinga and Łucja went to the Transfiguration Hospital and, with tears in their eyes, asked Sister Józefa for help (a Daughter of Charity of Saint Vincent de Paul, whose kindness they had experienced many times). She arranged the matter with the assistant professor of the second surgical clinic and they promised to admit Sister Bernadette on the following day.

In that hospital, Sister Bernadette was assigned to a room with four beds (room 22) and had a probe inserted into her stomach through her nose, to stop the vomiting. She was in good spirits and was making jokes. Drips of Cebion, glucose, and saline improved her appearance immediately. She said, "I am in paradise." She was soon visited by Professor Łapiński and Associate Professor Sadowski with a group of other doctors, and they diagnosed intestinal obstruction.

A second surgery was inevitable, but because of the patient's emaciation she had to be strengthened beforehand. On April 18 and 19, Sister Bernadette was given two liters of blood and intravenous nutrition. Someone was always by her side. Mrs. Wolska received a permanent day pass, and Sister Kinga was allowed to look after her at night. Sister Bernadette was calm and composed; she said, "They will take the lancet and cut." The surgery was performed on Saturday, April 23. It lasted four hours. Associate Professor Sadowski, the chief operating surgeon, admitted that the operation was extremely difficult. Twisted bowel, intestinal adhesions, pus, hematoma — none of that boded well. However, the surgery was successful.

The night after the surgery was full of tension. Even though the patient slept until midnight after an injection, when she woke up, she was very restless and agitated. She kept putting a damp cloth to her face, arms, and legs and saying, "Water is such a wonderful element." She repeated the praises of Sister Water, which is "humble and precious and pure," from the Canticle of the Sun by Saint Francis. During the night she got another analgesic injection, along with new drips and cardiac medication. However, at 4 A.M. Sister Bernadette's face became waxy, her chin drooped, and she developed cold sweats. The doctor on duty prescribed Corvin with caffeine. Her condition improved but she felt very weak. She would say that she had barely escaped death. She felt no hope of survival, but to spare her loved ones, especially her mother, she avoided the subject of death for the time being. She did her best to support the efforts of the doctors. She highly praised the medical and nursing care in the second hospital, especially that of Doctor Sadowski and Sister Józefa. "It was painful to look at the efforts of the doctors, nurses, and the monastery. . . . There was simply nothing left to grasp."[8]

Sister Bernadette was being kept alive with intravenous drips. Then she was allowed to drink bitter tea and even eat a little. However, under the watchful eye of the patient, it was more the nursing staff that took advantage of the supplied delicacies than the patient herself. Although she was starved to death and enjoyed every sip of milk or broth she swallowed, she could only take in small amounts of food.

The next five days (from April 22 to 26) were spent battling the disease, alternating between hope and despair of recovery. In fact, everything that was possible in this situation was done: blood transfusions, antibiotics, drips to strengthen the body. However, the doctors did not manage to make up for the negligence of their predecessors. Peritonitis developed. During the night of April 26 to 27, Sister Kinga concluded that the end was imminent and notified the monastery. The doctors decided to perform another very unpleasant procedure, but it turned out to be in vain. Her body was breaking down. Admittedly, even on Sunday, April 28, Professor Łapiński said, "We will get this girl out of this," but on the same day the patient was moved to the other side of the corridor, to the purulent ward. Further attempts to save her, including a variety of painful procedures, only caused more suffering.

The value of the body

She suffered greatly, and her words showed that the great cause for which she had willingly sacrificed her life never disappeared from the horizon of her soul. God did not abandon her either. In Sister Bernadette, the words of the Holy Scriptures were fulfilled, "O Lord God of heaven . . . have regard to the face of thy saints" (Jdt 6:19). Sister made an offering of the moral and physical sufferings of her

---

8   *Sister Kinga's Journal from the Time of the Final Illness of Sister Bernadette,* p. 28.

long illness for wayward souls among those who are consecrated to Him, for the sins they have committed with their body. That is why her own body became a burnt offering. Sister Kinga wrote:

> For the first time in my life I saw the immense value of the body in the service of God and its wonderful role as an instrument of the soul governing it. Everything that happened to Sister Bernadette's body and everything that I perceived in her soul seemed to be perfectly harmonized without a single false note.[9]

The patient's attitude toward death and suffering was extraordinary. During the whole period of her illness no attachment to life was observed in her. It is inevitable that her feelings fluctuated, but she always submitted herself to the will of God, however demanding it was. The patient rose above the physicians' attempts at solace; she dreamed of another life, one that is now almost forgotten. It is of that life that the Preface of the Mass for the Dead speaks so beautifully: *Tuis enim fidelibus, Domine, vita mutatur, non tollitur: et, dissoluta terrestris hujus incolatus domo, aeterna in caelis habitatio comparatur* (For to Thy faithful people, Lord, life is changed, not taken away; and when the home of this earthly sojourn is dissolved, an eternal dwelling is made ready in heaven).

Sister Bernadette showed a certain disregard for her own pain, which was so excruciating. During the final days and nights, already with burning bedsores on her back, she whimpered, "I would love to curl up in a ball and fall asleep." Sister Kinga, who already knew the "secret of the sacrifice" of Sister Bernadette from Mrs. Wolska, was overwhelmed by a strange feeling of God's watchful, jealous love. She did not wish to diminish in any way God's part in the mystery unfolding before her eyes. So she answered in an almost stern manner, "The Lord Jesus could not curl up in a ball and fall asleep on the Cross." Sister Bernadette responded admirably, "Exactly. The Lord Jesus could not have curled up on the Cross and fallen asleep." And then, with an air of remarkable disregard for her sufferings, she added, "Suffering, suffering . . ." Sister changed her strategy this time, "Well, you have your share with Him, and it is this that I envy you."

---

9   Ibid., p. 66.

Sister Bernadette replied with deep humility, "Yes, it is true, I have a share, but it is still a far cry from what He suffered..."

And yet she suffered greatly. "God really did take me at my word," she said at one point, writhing in pain between injections. At other times she would whisper, "I am lying here as if I were on fire." "She was so strong, so strong," Sister Kinga wrote.[10] However, there was no bravado in Sister Bernadette's attitude. She used anesthetics because Mother Celestyna asked that she be relieved from pain as much as possible. When she managed to sleep six hours during one night, in the morning she said, "Dear Pantopon.[11] I love it." She inquired, "Wouldn't you say that it makes no sense to ask someone to endure till the end?" Sister Kinga writes, "She treated her body and her resilience with reasonable, objective pity, with the same sound judgment that, along with her great patience, astounded the physicians."[12]

God can take what He pleases. Long intervals passed between the injections, the anesthetics were less and less effective, and successive procedures caused suffering. The veins, punctured by drips and injections became flaccid and would no longer accept anything more. These were times of excessive suffering.

On the eve of her death, one of the doctors told her to be patient and not to coddle herself. This was the only person on the medical staff who treated her with hostility. The only person, but not the only time. Sister Bernadette understood that God was not sparing her, as He did not spare His crucified Son, and she took this advice trying to find good will in it: "She is right! I must not coddle myself." The next day, during the doctor's rounds, she thanked her for it publicly and humbly, without a hint of malice.

For Sister Bernadette, her own pain did not obscure other people's suffering and exhaustion. At the sight of Sister Kinga's sacrifices, she said to her with solicitude, "It will be the end of you. Hard to tell who will be carried away first." Once she tried to kiss her hand. As always, she showed her gratitude for the services rendered to her. The presence of kind and loving people was no small consolation

---

10   *Sister Kinga's Journal*, p. 41.
11   The name of the painkiller medication.
12   *Sister Kinga's Journal*, p. 68.

Renamed outwardly turned

for her. She once said, "Mama is here, Sister Kinga is here, Lord
Jesus is here . . ." and, after a moment of silence, she added, "The
whole Holy Trinity. . ." A group of friends continued to visit her,
especially her dearest Sabina Czerniewska. Efforts were made to
give the dying woman comfort. Once they sent her bouquets of
the first marsh marigolds and campion flowers and, on the eve of
her death, anemones. Sister Bernadette had them placed on the
drip apparatus stand so she could look at them. She was no longer
afraid to see beauty in the world.

She knew that the sisters at the monastery, although absent in
the body, were surrounding her with prayer and thinking about her.
In the monastery, a telephone duty was established. Every update
about her was anticipated with fear, anxiety, and hope. Or rather,
since news of her sacrificial act had already begun to spread, "the
anticipation was full of a strange union with her. We knew that
some wonderful will and plan of God was being fulfilled, and at
the same time we all suffered with her."[13] When recounting her
feelings from those days, one of the sisters described them as "one
flame, one plea of my soul for this dear creature . . . . I begged God
not to let her leave His embrace even for a moment, to open heaven
to her directly." These feelings were shared by other sisters in the
monastery.

It so happened that the days of Sister Bernadette's agony, as
befits a Benedictine, were marked by wonderful liturgical texts:
April 29, for monastic Orders, is the feast of the Holy Abbots of
Cluny. The entrance antiphon of the Mass is "Come, ye blessed of
my Father, possess you the kingdom prepared for you from the
foundation of the world" (Mt 25:34). At Vespers, an antiphon[14]
was sung to the tune of the *Exsultet* about Saint Hugh, who died
while praising the paschal candle.

---

13   *Sister Kinga's Journal*, p. 48.
14   The text of the antiphon is: *Cum in die magni Sabbati beatus Hugo sacris
interesset, columnam novae lucis salutabat crebris exorans suspiriis, ut ad terram
promissionis feliciter perveniret, alleluia.* "While blessed Hugh was assisting at
the sacred mysteries on Holy Saturday, he saluted the column of new light
with repeated sighs, entreating that he might happily reach the land of promise,
alleluia."

Last visit of Mother Celestyna

On the same day, Sister Bernadette was visited by Mother Celestyna, who not only knew about her act of oblation, but as Prioress gave her consent to it. Mother was just about to attend a convention of superiors in Częstochowa, but she postponed it to render a final service to her spiritual daughter. She later described her last visit with Sister Bernadette. Upon entering the isolation room, she failed to recognize her, since Sister Bernadette had changed so much. With her closely-cropped hair she looked like a ten-year-old boy, her hands like two sticks. Sister Bernadette greeted the Prioress cordially, with the radiant smile of her final days. However, both Mother Celestyna and Sister Kinga had the impression that their presence was no longer necessary. Sister Bernadette was so immersed in God that everything besides Him was a pleasant but unnecessary bonus. Nevertheless, the visit proved to be providential. Only then did Sister Bernadette reveal the depth of her spiritual experiences. As we can conclude from her confessions, she had been in constant communion with the Lord throughout her stay in the Transfiguration Hospital, and it became ever more intense as death was approaching.

Sister Bernadette repeated the words that determined her fate: "Cut me into strips, but let them return to You and give You glory." With a triumphant smile she threw back the quilt to show how literally those words were fulfilled. Her poor emaciated body had been cut in different directions. At the bottom, where the incision from the first surgery met the one from the second surgery, a cavity had been left for the pus to drain out, and above that a few stitches were still holding. Above them a cavity had formed where some stitches had come apart. The patient saw this as a sign that God would also grant the second part of her request.

She confided, "You know, Mother, how enormously simple God is, and death is so simple, and I have become so simple, and in this wonderful simplicity of God I am so happy." Mother admitted that she could tell her recent progress in this virtue. "Yes," replied Sister Bernadette,

> but during these two months in the hospital, especially since this experience with God, strangely all difficulties and problems have fallen away — nothing bothers me anymore.

A photograph taken of Mother Celestyna in the 1960s.

I am just extremely happy. I am happy that I am going to die. Oh, how immensely I long for death! It is unspeakable, I want so much to be with Him already.... I can feel it, He also wants to tear down the veil, but I do not know who wants it more. He is here, He no longer leaves me at all, He is always with me. I don't pray like that, no, I don't think so, but we love each other.[15]

When Mother Celestyna expressed sympathy with her sufferings, Sister Bernadette reassured her:

But that is not at all why I want to die; suffering is also a great happiness. I want to suffer as much as possible for a few more moments, there is no more suffering there . . . I feel a great power inside me. It is not from me, but from Him. I understand the martyrs. You know, Mother, it's as if I were walking straight into the Divine Light by some great impulse of the Holy Spirit. You know that during those twelve years of religious life I had some very beautiful and joyful moments, so many of them, but they do not compare at all with the happiness that is flooding me now. It has something of eternity in it.[16]

The conversation was interrupted by one of the doctors who entered and leaned over the patient's bed with concern. "It hurts a lot here, doctor" (on another occasion she had said that the pain there was "more and more aggressive"). The doctor grimaced and whispered, "Peritoneum," asked a few questions, and left the room. Mother Celestyna asked what the conversation was about. Sister Bernadette laughed, "I wasn't listening at all. I know I'm going to die, and that's all that matters to me, not things which are so trivial and not worth dwelling upon."[17]

Their farewell was both cordial and moving. Tears welled up in Sister Bernadette's eyes when the Prioress blessed her for her passage into eternity. It was their last visit because the next day, prompted by a phone call from Częstochowa, Mother Celestyna had to leave.

Sister Bernadette was not able to receive Holy Communion for a

---

15 *Journals of Mother Celestyna Wielowieyska.*
16 Ibid.; last sentence according to witnesses' recollections.
17 Ibid.

long time because of her vomiting. Before leaving, Mother Celestyna expressed her wish that Sister should not be deprived of the Holy Viaticum, also because of the charism of the Benedictine Nuns of the Blessed Sacrament, and asked Sister Kinga to take care of that, especially since the vomiting had stopped. Sister Józefa saw no reason to rush and recommended postponing the Holy Communion till the morning, since Sister Bernadette was in constant spiritual contact with Christ. Although Sister Bernadette longed for the sacramental meeting with the Lord, she agreed to this solution, taking it almost as a question of honor that her will be broken: "That is fine, then." Sister Kinga, however, saw no reason to yield and asked for the Viaticum in an adamant tone. The chaplain agreed immediately, but Sister Kinga had the impression that he did so not because of her insistence, but because he saw Sister Bernadette's resignation.

"I am the bread of life. This is the bread which cometh down from heaven; that if any man eat of it, he may not die" (Jn 6:48-50). A drawing from The Mass of a Soul.

O Rex Gloriae

This Holy Communion proved to be a providential reinforcement before the nightmarish night awaiting the sick one. Although Sister Bernadette fell asleep for a while after the Pantopon, the anesthetics had little effect. She woke up around 11:30 P.M. Sore, she complained, "This is the bottom, the bottom . . . I cannot do it anymore, I really cannot pretend anymore in front of my mother. . . . I'm crying out so much, Sister, crying out so much." Sister Kinga then reminded her of Christ crying out in Gethsemane, with whom she must have a share. Sister Bernadette's words, "I cannot," along with heroic patience, completed her conformity with the Crucified One.

As the nurse responsible for the sick sister's condition, Sister Kinga had to help. Sister Bernadette could no longer find a comfortable position that would not cause her pain. Since the needle was out of the vein and the hand was blue and cold, Sister Kinga placed the drip into the other hand. When she realized after an hour that the other hand was not absorbing anything either, she removed the drip in order not to torment the patient unnecessarily. The pulse could not be taken; in the morning the fever chart showed almost 108 degrees Fahrenheit. Sister Kinga could feel through her habit and nurse's apron that the patient's body was like a hot iron. Bringing her some relief was all that could have been done. That very night, the doctor who was hostile towards Sister Bernadette was on duty, and so all requests fell on deaf ears. In the morning, between 3 A.M. and 6:30 A.M., Sister Bernadette's face began to change, but the doctor concluded that it was just ordinary morning fatigue. However, it was already her agony. At 4:20 A.M., Sister Kinga called the monastery and Mrs. Wolska to inform them that the end was near. Sister Bernadette received Holy Communion for the last time. She did not hide her feelings. She said that she could still hear in her heart the triumphant melody of the antiphon *O Rex gloriae*, although she could not remember the words. She was referring to the Magnificat antiphon of Second Vespers for the feast of the Ascension: "O King of glory, Lord of hosts, Who hast this day mounted in triumph above all the heavens, leave us not orphans: but send unto us the promise of the Father, the Spirit of truth, alleluia." When Sister Kinga asked what she should say to the Prioress, she heard, "Just this: *O Rex gloriae, Christe*."

It was the feast of Saint Catherine of Siena, who for Sister Bernadette was a saint of great wisdom who made her death a holocaust for the Church. Today, the commemoration of this saint, proclaimed a Doctor of the Church in 1970, has its own Mass formulary with different prayers, and her memorial is celebrated on April 29.[18] At that time, the monastery sang the poignantly beautiful antiphon for Communion, *Quinque prudentes virgines*, referring to Matthew's par-

Ad Magnificat, Antiphona. II D

The antiphon O Rex gloriae as found in the 1934 Antiphonale Monasticum, the edition from which Sister Bernadette most likely sang this antiphon. (Image: © Abbaye Saint-Pierre de Solesmes)

able of the wise and foolish virgins (cf. Mt 25:1–13). The translation of the antiphon reads: "The five wise virgins took oil in their vessels with the lamps; and at midnight there was a cry made: 'Behold, the Bridegroom cometh: go ye forth to meet Christ the Lord!'" And the Secret includes this petition: "May our prayers and this saving Victim,

18   As mentioned before, April 29 in the monastic calendar was (and, in some places, still is) the feast of Saints Odo, Majolus, Odilo, and Hugh; at that time, Saint Catherine was celebrated on April 30.

fragrant with virginal sweetness, which we offer Thee on this festival of blessed Catherine, ascend unto Thee, O Lord."

Sister Kinga remembered Mother Celestyna's warning that amidst the abundance of graces, some anxiety could also appear, and that the anxiety before death could sometimes be terrifying. Therefore, when Sister Bernadette said, "I have adored so little . . ." and asked her guardian to help her apologize to God for all her faults, Sister Kinga, in order to protect her from those anxieties, decided that reciting two verses of the *Miserere* (Psalm 50) would be enough and quite firmly reminded the dying woman of the obligation to forget herself, even her own death, because Christ was adored in her and He was the only one who counted. Sister Bernadette agreed, "Yes, only God is important." The anxiety disappeared. They recited the Magnificat together. Sister Bernadette asked if they could also recite the *Te Deum*, but her exhausted nurse could not remember the words, so they fell silent for a while.

Then Sister Bernadette kept repeating, "The eye hath not . . . nor ear" (cf. 1 Cor 2:9), and, "Please, Sister, use your influence 'there' so that He will take me sooner." The wonderful antiphon about the glorious fulfillment of the mission of Christ the Redeemer kept resounding in her heart.

We should devote a few words to her heroic mother. Mrs. Wolska stood by her daughter, taking the attitude of the mother of the seven sons described in the Second Book of Maccabees, and she kept renewing the sacrifice she had already made of her most beloved child. Suffering as only a mother can suffer, she neither shed vain tears nor complained. In the morning, she sometimes greeted her daughter with just a glance, because Sister Bernadette did not always have the strength to whisper, "Mama," and then with an impressive calmness she would get down to tending to her. She accepted her daughter's act of oblation. On the morning of the day Sister Bernadette died, April 30, Sister Kinga whispered to Mrs. Wolska, "Let's give her up." Sister Bernadette encompassed them both with a look: "Mama gave up her child, she did. She said, 'Take the child, take the child.'" Mrs. Wolska repeated, "Yes, take the child." Both were filled with extraordinary peace and the presence of grace was palpable.

Then the dying woman was once again tormented by vomiting. She tried to sit up, and a moment later, completely exhausted, she would say, "I must lie down! I must lie down now!" She collapsed on the bed. In leaning to her right side, she resembled Saint Thérèse of the Child Jesus and Saint Elizabeth of the Trinity, who both died in this posture. Sister Kinga was standing there in helpless desperation, awaiting the inevitable. However, Sister Józefa showed up with an injection and a dressing for the abdomen. In the meantime, Doctor Sadowski had arrived and continued trying to save the sick woman, against all hope. Sister Józefa would attempt to persuade him, "Why should we make her suffer more?" but her pleas were ineffective. Sister Bernadette herself also said, "Dear doctor, it's not worth it anymore, my veins can't take anything more. I want to go to heaven," but the doctor kept trying. A pointless venesection was performed. The vein in her right arm, lacerated by drips and injections, was surgically extracted with instruments and replaced with a catheter. She was given glucose and neoadrenaline, oxygen was administered through the nose, and a probe was inserted into the stomach to pump out its horrible contents. High doses of heart medication and painkillers were administered. The only positive result of all that was that Sister Bernadette was able to recognize her own sister, Joanna Plewińska, who had arrived in the morning from Cracow, summoned by her mother's phone call. Looking at her sister's devastated body, she whispered, "Auschwitz." Sister Bernadette was delighted to see her. Both Joanna and her mother warmed up in their hands Sister Bernadette's feet and hands, which were cool to the touch. The dying woman asked for orange juice, but after a while, she changed her mind, "Let's not waste the oranges." When the nurse arrived with a painkiller injection, she protested, "What's the point?" But when Sister Kinga explained to her that by doing the Prioress's will, she would be fulfilling the final act of obedience, she brightened up, "The final act of obedience!" and protested no more. Sister Kinga was sent back to the monastery to get some rest before the expected hardships of the following night. The patient herself was the most persuasive, "Please go, somehow I am still not dead, although the dress rehearsal has already taken place."

Into Thy hands I commend my spirit

Sister Kinga's rest was not long. Between eleven and twelve she was called back to the hospital. Sister Bernadette was no longer in pain. Half-sitting, leaning against the pillows, she fell into a deep, pre-mortem sleep. She still had drains, a probe, and a drip. She was being kept alive artificially.

The agony started at 2 P.M. It was witnessed by Sister Bernadette's mother, her sister Joanna Plewińska with her husband, and by Sister Kinga, Sister Łucja, and Sister Magdalena from the monastery community. Three other patients from the same room were crying and praying as they watched the dying sister. Sister Józefa lit the candle which Mrs. Wolska held in her Rozmarynka's cooling hand. Sister Bernadette was unconscious. Her pulse was no longer detectable, and her lungs were functioning with growing difficulty. At first, the dying woman was whispering indistinctly two words, "God" and "Mama." At times she only moaned. Sister Kinga began the prayers for the dying, and then the antiphon *O Rex gloriae*, which triumphantly opened heaven for the dying woman.

Together they recited Psalm 90, *Qui habitat in adjutorio Altissimi*. At three o'clock in the afternoon, Sister Bernadette breathed her last. First Vespers of the feast of Saint Joseph was being chanted in the monastery at that time. The hymn *Te, Joseph, celebrant agmina caelitum* (Joseph! To Thee by Hosts on High) ends with words that were particularly fitting for that moment:

> Spare us, O Trinity most High!
> Grant that, with Joseph, we may gain
> Thy starry realm, and ceaselessly
> There raise to Thee our thankful strain.[19]

During the singing of the Magnificat, the sister on telephone duty inched open the door to the choir and gave a sign which was noticed by most of the nuns. At the conclusion of Vespers, the hebdomadarian officially announced to the community that Sister Bernadette had died. The news was expected at any moment and greeted with prayer and tears, which were not bitter. The sisters were overwhelmed with a

---

19   *Nobis, summa Trias, parce precantibus, / Da Joseph meritis sidera scandere; / Ut tandem liceat nos tibi perpetim / Gratum promere canticum.*

Sister Bernadette of the Cross in death.

wonderful feeling that one of them, the most privileged and mature one, had just attained the fullness of God's life. However, Sister Bernadette's death really distressed the doctors, especially Professor Łapiński and Doctor Sadowski. The former said to Sister Józefa on the following day, "I can't cope with it, I'm so upset by the death of that sister. She was so quiet, so pleasant, so intelligent, and so young." These feelings were shared by Doctor Sadowski, who directly took care of Sister Bernadette and who did everything in his power to save her.

However, the sisters in the monastery were saddened by the news that Sister Bernadette's body could not be released until May 2, because the hospital administration was closed. Nevertheless, thanks to many efforts, her body arrived at the monastery at 6 P.M. The sisters gathered at the cloister gate welcomed it with great emotion. The grandeur of death was so palpable that it seemed as if the Sister, like the high priest of the Old Covenant, wore on her forehead a plate engraved with the words, "Holy to the Lord," (Ex 28:36). She was wholly and forever His. Someone told the Prioress that if a contemplative monastery raises even one such soul, it has fulfilled its purpose. Upon her return from Częstochowa, Mother Celestyna approached Sister Bernadette's bier and kissed her emaciated hand reverently. Following the custom of the monastery, the sisters took turns at the coffin, reciting the Psalter. The next day, a joyful Mass of Saint Joseph was sung: "Our soul waiteth for the Lord: for he is our helper and protector. For in him our heart shall rejoice: and in his holy name we have trusted" (Ps 32:20–21). The whole day was spent in prayer. Family, friends, and representatives of the monasteries of the Institute arrived. The funeral was set for the following day, May 2. God saw to it that the liturgical texts were fitting for the passing of Sister Bernadette. The morning Mass for the feast of Saint Athanasius had a proper reading from the Second Epistle to the Corinthians (2 Cor 4:6–14):

> For God, who commanded the light to shine out of darkness, hath shined in our hearts, to give the light of the knowledge of the glory of God, in the face of Christ Jesus .... Knowing that he who raised up Jesus, will raise us up also with Jesus, and place us with you.

The priests chanted the Office for the Dead. After the Holy Sacrifice of the Mass was offered, in accordance with the privilege accorded to Benedictine Nuns of the Blessed Sacrament, the Mother Prioress covered Sister Bernadette's face with the corporal of her funeral Mass. The sisters took the coffin on their shoulders and carried it to the crypt of the church where the nuns were buried. It was an altogether lovely day in May. To conclude the funeral rites, First Vespers of the Solemnity of Our Lady Queen of Poland were sung. She was honored with the verses of the beautiful hymn *Ave, maris stella*:

> Virgin all excelling,
> Mildest of the mild,
> Free from guilt preserve us
> Meek and undefiled.
>
> Keep our life all spotless,
> Make our way secure
> Till we find in Jesus,
> Joy for evermore.[20]

---

20   *Virgo singularis, / inter omnes mites, / nos culpis solutos, / mitis fac et castos.*
Vitam praesta puram, / iter para tutum: / ut videntes Jesum / semper collaetemur.

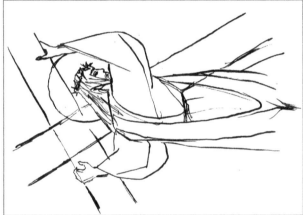

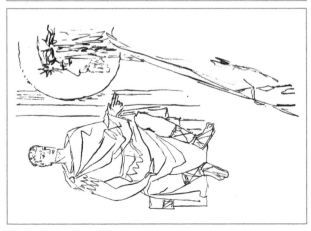

A Way of the Cross, drawn by Sister Bernadette for a relative who was in hospital.

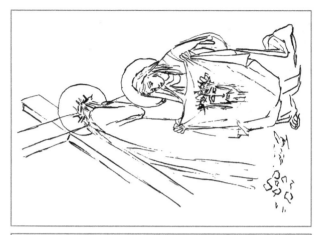

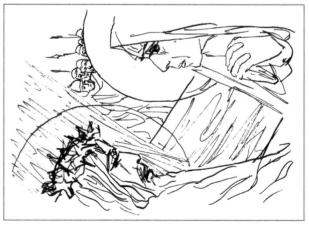

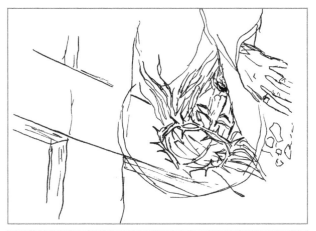

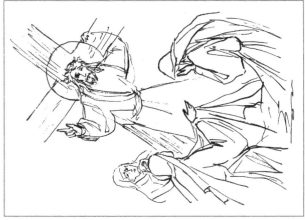

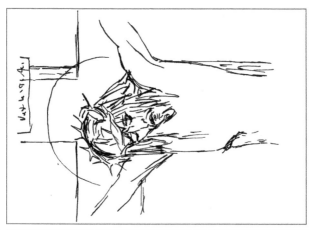

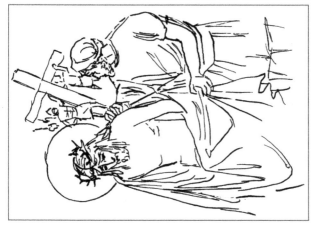

To what purpose was this waste?

Sister Bernadette's death reminded the sisters of her community of the dignity and greatness of their vocation — "Thou hast multiplied thy wonderful works, O Lord my God: and in thy thoughts there is no one like to thee" (Ps 39:6) — but also of the rigor of God's demands: "For every one shall be salted with fire" (Mk 9:48). The question of sin today has been mocked and pushed to the margins of life, yet sin demands reparation, and even more so the sins of priests who are daily in contact with what is most sacred. After all, the Lord said to Aaron, "Thou and thy sons with thee shall bear the sins of your priesthood" (Nm 18:1).

For every sin, the price to be paid is death. Most of all, the death of Christ washes away sin. In the New Covenant there is a miraculous law of substitution, in imitation of Christ Himself. The blood of the Church is mixed, through His graciousness, with the Blood of the Savior. Sister Bernadette's act is one of a series of sacrificial offerings made for priests, especially by cloistered nuns, although many priests do not understand the nuns' vocation. Sister Bernadette once wrote down the words of Saint John Chrysostom addressed to a Christian virgin: "He gave His Blood for you, you owe Him blood" — and she lived them out to the end.

As it does for every deceased sister, the Community offered thirty Masses, the so-called Gregorian Masses, for Sister Bernadette, and prayed the prayers recommended by the monastery constitutions. Most of the sisters prayed not so much for her as for her intercession.

For a whole month, a crucifix placed in the refectory in Sister Bernadette's seat was a reminder of her. Then her personal belongings went into general use; every sister wanted to have something of hers as a relic. The memory of her humble holiness and holocaust was perpetuated and remained alive in the community. The news about her spread widely. In an extensive letter of May 25, 1963, Mother Celestyna described all the events to Stefan Cardinal Wyszyński, the Primate of Poland. The story was shared with relatives and friends. This sincere interest is the reason for this book, a testimony that may be helpful to modern people.

Father Piotr Rostworowski wrote to Mrs. Wolska:

Our Rozmarynka has flown to heaven, leaving us in sorrow.
I understand it all the more deeply, because she was also my
child, and, in some way, I miss her. On the other hand, the
departure of such a soul has something of God's peace in
it; it bestows peace on those who remain.... God knows
why he demanded this immolation.[21]

Much like Sister Bernadette's contemplative life, and perhaps
even more so, her oblation may not seem purposeful, necessary, or
meaningful to everyone. Many will ask, as they once did at the sight
of Mary of Bethany, anointing Jesus' feet with a precious oil: "To
what purpose is this waste?" (Mt 26:8). But God should be offered
that which is the most precious. Such was Sister Bernadette's gift,
consisting of her own life, being a part of God's *mysterium*. Therefore,
Christ's blessing also applies to her: "Let her alone, why do you molest
her? She hath wrought a good work upon me" (Mk 14:6).

---

21   Letter of May 5, 1963.

PART 2
A Selection
of
Sister Bernadette's
Writings

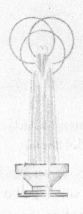

IN FESTO
SS-me TRINITATIS

ORATIO

Omnipótens sempitérne Deus, qui dedisti fámulis tuis in confessióne vere fídei, aetérnae Trinitátis glóriam ag-nóscere, et in poténtia majestátis adoráre Unitátem:* quaésumus; ut, ejusdem fídei firmitáte,* ab ómnibus semper muniámur advérsis. Per Dominum nostrum...

Another page from Sister Bernadette's Evangeliarium.

1
Excerpts from Letters to Her Mother

The breviary is a gold mine

We have already traveled quite a bit during these three weeks, and so much has happened on the way that it is hard to decide what to talk about. In any case, during that time the most important were the holy days (Pentecost, Trinity Sunday, and Corpus Christi) in their entire span, that is, including the vigils and octaves.[1] In fact, it is only now, thanks to the breviary, among other things, that I have discovered these holy days. I didn't appreciate them at all before. In general, the breviary is a gold mine!

Another important matter—the visit of the Primate, he himself and the things he said. He spoke about the Holy Father, from whom he brought us a blessing, about Blessed [now Saint] Pius X (the Pope of the Most Holy Eucharist), that we should pray to him, because he is a mighty intercessor with God, and that he is like a tree with ripe fruit, so it is enough just to walk under it, and the fruit falls down. The sisters asked in unison what they should pray for, to which the Primate replied that they should pray only for holiness. He spoke about Monte Cassino and about the bones of Saint Benedict and Saint Scholastica, which have been buried together up till this point and which the doctors are now trying to identify and separate with great effort. All this in a few simple and warm words. Truly, it was no small thing, I am telling you, dear Mama. All the plaster and molding suddenly disappeared and you could only feel what was underneath: the living organism of the Church, her simple unity, a real and living bond with the Holy Father.

May 23, 1951

---

1   The octave of Corpus Christi, among others, was suppressed in 1955, and that of Pentecost in 1969, but some communities continue to celebrate some of these octaves in one form or another. The whole Octave of Corpus Christi also continues to be observed in Poland up to the present day.

So I don't forget how people painted

I have to "set myself up" for working in my profession [as an artist]. It's going to be quite difficult, because the work itself is always difficult for me, but on top of that, there is the difficulty of satisfying the clients and, at the same time, making sure that these things are at least harmless. However, I should look at something from time to time, so that I don't forget how people painted. And that's why I'm asking you to send me some of the materials I used to have.

June 1, 1951

I'm not worried because that would be rude

I do not know how you are doing, dear Mama, but we have Providence on which the smallest things depend, so even more these [greater] ones. And Providence likes to have a person hang on by a thread and ask for everything, and believe that he or she will receive it, so I am not worried, because that would be rude. One should always be rejoicing, and it is *possible*, as you have surely experienced many times, dear Mama, and that is wonderful. It is precisely such "hopeless" moments that can be worth something. And since you are not short of such moments, it is better to be happy than to worry. Am I right? At such times there is nothing like the Psalms! I am sure you think so too, dear Mama.

February 26, 1952

There is no use worrying about anyone

The consolation in this is that Providence watches over every man and nothing escapes it. Every little thing is governed with great precision, which can sometimes be seen ten years later, if at all. I have arrived at the conclusion that there is no use worrying about anyone, because all this governing is, fortunately, not our responsibility, and if it does depend on us in any way, it would probably be only through our prayers.

July 21, 1952

Tricentennial celebrations

Beginning with the Annunciation, we had a triduum for the tricentennial [of the Institute], which consisted of an all-day Exposition [of the Blessed Sacrament], Solemn Masses celebrated by the

Bishops, and on the last day by the Cardinal, who not only spoke as he alone can do, but came to us, saw the exhibit, and later, when he was leaving, he turned around once again, sat down, and asked us to "sing him something Gregorian."

He said that in three hundred years surely none of us would be in purgatory, and he was extremely happy about that, because it will be so soon.

March 30, 1953

When you get to know the will of God

I know that the yellow notebook[2] is a very good notebook and I am glad that you have it, dear Mama, and that you have Father Wojtyła for spiritual matters. It is so important that you have someone to lean on in all your troubles, because you know that he will always advise you wisely and according to God's way. And when you get to know the will of God, then even if on the outside nothing works out and it goes against the grain, you can still enjoy true peace in the depths of your soul, which, it seems to me, is a very important good for the soul, and which is worth "seeking and pursuing," as our *Holy Rule* says [in the Prologue].

April 26, 1953

Time no longer belongs to me, but to someone else

So much has happened that I do not know where to begin. I should probably start by saying that I feel "starved" and for a long time I have been writing letters to you "by spiritual mail," dear Mama, because I didn't have the time to write ordinary letters. That, by the way, is not surprising, because time no longer belongs to me, but to someone else, just like everything else contained in it. And when you begin to miss letters from me, dear Mama, please console yourself with the thought of the tabernacle; we can meet wonderfully and truly there, not to mention in Holy Communion.

October 2, 1953, Feast of the Holy Guardian Angels

---

2   A coincidental similarity of name with the yellow notebook of Saint Thérèse of the Child Jesus.

It is so real and alive

My "I don't have the time" has a different meaning than it does in the world because I really don't have anything anymore and I am dead in a way, because I don't belong to myself anymore since my vows. Mama, how wonderful it all is, because it is so real and alive. In fact, we all legally belong to Him, but the happiest are those who want to belong to Him and who want to exist only in Him. All the texts of today's feast show this truth wonderfully. I don't know if it is ever possible for a person to appreciate even a little bit what a blessing it is to be a member of Christ's Church. In this life, probably not. We are not fit to understand anything at all in this life, and we would save ourselves a lot of distress if we simply believed. You know, dear Mama, for me every act of faith is still a new lesson that this is the only way for us, and that only by believing can we get closer to God.

October 25, 1953, Feast of Christ the King

Look at the Immaculate

We celebrated the Immaculate Conception as solemnly as possible throughout the entire octave.[3] On the feast itself, Father[4] presided at both Vespers and Lauds, which made it even more festive. In the morning, he preached a homily on Our Lady and the Jubilee Year.[5] I have it written down, but I won't have the time to transcribe it for you for a while. I only remembered that in this Jubilee Year we should expect an even greater increase of Satan's influence, because the battle with the Serpent is ongoing, but we are to lean on her power and grace, because we do not have the strength on our own, and, relying on her, we should decide not to give in to any compromises. And I also remember that we are simply to look to her and thus become better and purer. And that nowadays it is so difficult to explain to young people the need for the virtue of chastity, but when you put the Blessed Mother before their eyes, they begin to understand and it becomes obvious to them . . . "Look at the Immaculate, and it becomes clear."

December 17, 1953

---

3   As mentioned in an earlier note, many octaves were abolished in 1955, including that of the Immaculate Conception mentioned here.

4   Piotr Rostworowski, OSB.

5   This was the first Marian year in history, proclaimed to celebrate the centenary of the promulgation of the dogma of the Immaculate Conception.

QUE SOY ERA IMMACULADA COUNCEPCIOU

IN ASSUMPTIONE B.M.V.

ORATIO.

Omnípotens sempitérne Deus, qui imma-
culátam Vírginem Maríam, Fílii tui
Genitrícem, córpore et ánima ad coe-
léstem glóriam assumpsisti:*concede
quaesumus; ut ad superna semper in-
tenti* ipsius gloriae mereamur esse
consortes. Per eumdem Dominum...

Sister Bernadette has added Our Lady's words to Saint Bernadette at Lourdes to her depiction of the Immaculate Conception in the Evangeliarium.

Sadness proves that one is not yet a sincere friend of the Cross

At our place there was a lot to be done before Easter, more than is normal in the world, but it is so arranged that it is accomplished with a peculiar harmony and beauty. I think the main reason for this is that a religious community is a supernatural institution.

During Easter I may get around to writing, but today I will only write that which is most necessary. First, I would like to wish you, dear Mama, the fullest possible experience of Holy Week, so that the *Alleluia* will be all the more joyful. For I find that sadness (except for repentance of heart, which is pleasing sadness) proves that one is not yet a sincere friend of the Cross, and a cheerfulness that does not come from carrying the Cross well is at least uncertain. Don't you think so, Mama? So that's what I wish for you and for myself as well, that is, that friendship with the Cross of Christ and the joy it brings. On Palm Sunday, Father N. was here and for an hour and a half he showed us slides of the Shroud of Turin, which coincided with our last fascinating but shocking reading: *A Doctor at Calvary: The Passion of Our Lord Jesus Christ as Described by a Surgeon*, by Pierre Barbet, based, among other things, on the Shroud of Turin in the light of the most recent research.

Holy Tuesday, 1954

It is not worth complaining to anyone else

In the last letter I rejoiced most of all [with] "perfect joy" that you, dear Mama, went to complain to the Lord Jesus, because it is not worth it to complain to anyone else — and the fact that there is something to complain about is foreseen by Him in every detail. The only thing is to do everything together with Him.

May 2, 1954

So much can be gained and so much lost

We witnessed the exhumation of our [sisters] killed during the Warsaw Uprising (they are the ones who sacrificed themselves).[6] You can probably imagine what it was like for us, especially now. Not counting the other spiritual blessings that we received on that occasion, this meditation alone, done in solitude, over those blackened skulls and skeletons (September 5, 1954) was incredibly important to me.[7] It was an encounter with eternity as something

---

6   At least seventeen of the thirty-four nuns who were killed when the monastery was bombed by the Germans during the Warsaw Uprising on August 31, 1944, had come quietly to the Prioress, Mother Janina, to obtain her permission to offer their lives. One sister captured the essence of this act best when she said that "sacrifices needed to be made so that Poland will belong to nobody but Christ." This sacrificial offering and terrible carnage became widely known in Poland, and is justly regarded as one of the most moving events in the history of Mother Mectilde's spiritual daughters.

7   Some initial exhumations and reburial occurred in April 1945, and as excavations and rebuilding progressed in the years following the war, additional

A moment of prayer during the exhumations.

very real and close. When you look at these human remains in such a way, you see the meaning of life. Everything falls away and only one thing remains — that which was for God and in God, because only that is eternal. Everything else is nothingness. And this life of ours, in which so much can be gained and so much lost, is so frighteningly short and fragile that we really should not waste any time. This meditation gave me the impetus to approach matters with courage. A Christian does not fear death, even the worst death, if every day already in this life he trains himself to die to himself and "hateth his life in this world" (Jn 12:25). When all this appeared so very clear and real to me in those days, I prayed a lot for my parents and siblings, and for everyone. For only the Lord God can enlighten man.

September 12, 1954

---

discovery and identification of various bodies were made. On Easter Tuesday, 1947, the tabernacle and ciborium containing the Blessed Sacrament around which the nuns had perished was discovered. When the church had been rebuilt, the nuns, after much resistance from the government, were able to make a complete exhumation of the reburied nuns in 1954 and inter them in the rebuilt church's vault. It is this latter event that is referred to in Sister Bernadette's letter.

"Thou wouldest not" is the whole tragedy

I was reading Saint Paul's Epistle to the Hebrews the other day; perhaps you will find, dear Mama, that it would be a good thing to give it to Wanda. It occurred to me that it would be good to do that. The Gospel from the Feast of Saint Stephen made me understand that the Lord Jesus is powerless, in a way, when a soul explicitly rejects Him. And that led Him to weep — Him! That "and thou wouldest not?" [Mt 23:37] is the whole tragedy. This matter has been on my heart and, to a certain extent, also on my conscience, and that's why I won't write too much about it, so that my duties don't suffer...

I would write to you, dear Mama, about Christmas, if it were possible, but an ink that would be fitting for the task has not yet been invented.

December 26th, 1954

What we do only matters on whether God wants it or not

I remember to take Cebion every other day. I don't know if it's a good system, but I think I'm not exaggerating if I say that I have a lot to do, especially as we are getting closer to Easter. It takes fifteen minutes just to read the listings of the Holy Week chants, and much longer to learn them. I am counting on the help of Saint Cecilia[8] as I have just finished painting her picture. The next orders are Christ the King and Saint Pius X and so on. I am doing my best so that these paintings do not offend God, and I comfort myself with the fact that what we do is not important in itself, and only matters depending on whether God wants it or not.

Apart from that, together with the sister in charge of the sacristy, I am decorating Christ's tomb[9] in our church. The main idea is that there should be no unnecessary distractions, only the "naked truth" prompting us to pray and not to look around. There will be a cross covered with blood as depicted in the Holy Shroud, an altar with a monstrance and a chalice under it, a statue of the Lord Jesus covered with the shroud under the mensa. Under the arms of the

---

8   The patron saint of music.
9   There is a tradition in Poland of preparing and decorating Christ's tomb (Polish: *Grób Pański*) on Good Friday. The Blessed Sacrament is placed there, along with a figure of Christ and various decorations. Churches remain open all night, and the faithful pray at the tomb and adore the Blessed Sacrament.

cross, an inscription from Saint Paul, "Thou hast redeemed us by Thy Blood."[10] It should be good.

March 31, 1955

Like His own Son

That which comes from the will of God does not depress a person, because one knows that it is coming from the hand of the most tender of fathers. And even that which is very painful speaks more clearly of the love He has for us, because through it all, He wants to make us like His own Son. *Plus tout nous manque sur la terre, plus nous trouvons ce que la terre peut nous donner de meilleur: la Croix* [The more we lack everything on earth, the more we find the best that the earth can give us: the Cross] — [Blessed] Charles de Foucauld.

If you managed to make it to the Shrine of the Black Madonna, dear Mama, then Our Lady was not stingy, because she can't be that. I was enormously happy at the thought that you would be there and would pray for all of us and thank her on my behalf!

And I had a retreat for three more days, and today it seems to me that two years have passed, not two weeks, because they were so spacious. God is very good indeed.

December 18, 1955

Worth a hundred worlds and a hundred joys?

Our happiness is not supposed to be here on earth and I think that everything that God is sending you now, dear Mama, is supposed to help us in this complete "adjustment," so that we do not take anything from this life and from this world except the Cross, and so that we do not want to take anything else. It is only a matter of praying unceasingly for this grace above all graces, so as to truly find in the Cross the joy that it contains, in the face of which all the joys that a "happy" life can offer a person are dung [cf. Phil 3:8]. I promise to double my supplications for this grace for you, dear Mama, and for myself, and I am also asking you to do the same. It seems to me that it is a great honor for you that the Lord Jesus has been sending you such trials to test your love and trust in Him. In fact, it is the greatest trial there could be. I am going to beg Him for strength for you and the grace you need to gladly give everything to Him, and

---

10   She is actually referring to Rv 5:9.

that He Himself may be your great reward [cf. Mt 5:12]. Mama! Is
not Our Lord Jesus worth a hundred worlds and a hundred earthly
joys? But nothing will help here, no words, only prayer and grace.

September 19, 1956

An invaluable discovery

Dear Mama, I must share with you an invaluable discovery when
it comes to working on improving ourselves. So, this whole bundle
of vices and abominations — this is precisely the very magnet that
draws our Redeemer towards us. If we attempt to cover our sores and
rags [cf. Lk 16:20] with a good impression, with some of our own
decency and "righteousness," the Good Samaritan [cf. Lk 10:25–37]
may pass us by, seeing that we do not need him. My conclusion is a
great joy and serenity at the sight of this filth in us, "which merited
such and so great a Redeemer" [*Exsultet*] and at the thought that
the more severe and terrible the disease, the greater the glory of the
physician who cured it. Does it also delight and comfort you as it
does me, dear Mama?

February 13, 1958

What about the Heavenly Mother?

I am feeling so much better now than I did during your stay,
dear Mama, and perhaps the Lord will grant that I should be well
by August. After all that you have done for me here, I thought to
myself that if an earthly mother can work "miracles" for her children,
then what about the Heavenly Mother? Your recent visit, Mama,
has greatly increased my love for her. I feel that it is providential
and that only she can trample the head of my self-love, which has
at least seven such heads.

June 1, 1958

Suggesting a good thing shatters freedom

"Rushing" someone, especially in the religious sphere, only triggers a
spirit of contrariness, and often I would already have done something
on my own, but the moment a third person, even if it is someone near
and dear, steps in between my good will and some divine command, it
disastrously shatters my being "one on one" with that command. This
"one on one" is very delicate and precious, because it alone creates the
atmosphere in which a person can act freely, and it is freedom that

gives savor to our actions. You have to be very accomplished to take the shortest route in following the objective and apprehended good, and not pay any attention to whether someone's intervention spoiled your taste and joy of freedom of choice and action, because the good itself attracts you. But as long as this good has not yet completely conquered the soul, and as long as it has not yet fully captivated and conquered her, it is only by prayer and example that one can contribute to this. Until the fish "begins to bite," no one picks up the rod, and, as Abbé Pierre [Grouès] says,[11] grain will not grow any faster if you pull the grass. I would be delighted if you were to find these things true, Mama! If that were the case, and if you found it to be useful and practical, I can imagine how much such "restraint" might often cost you. But I can vouch for the fact that such a method will be more suitable and effective, and at the same time more deserving before God, because it is altruistic. I trust that you will forgive me this "sermon," but . . . what I wrote to you [above] — these are the keys which may help a little in fishing out young souls for God.

July 1, 1958

The last drop of life

Wishing "a hundred years"[12] is atrociously stingy and . . . I only wish him that as a humble supplement . . . . Time runs so fast, and with it our life is leaking like water from a jug with a hole, and that's why the best wish is that the last drop may be charged with God's grace and love.

September 24, 1958

Tension . . . and embroidery

Various strange things have been happening at our house. Reverend Mother was away for a few days for a convention of superiors, and besides that, we have been living in constant tension because of the new foundation in Siedlce, which is being born in pain and cannot be born. I am asking you, dear Mama, to please pray for this

---

11   Sister Bernadette seems to reference this quote as coming from "od łachmaniarzy." The editors were unable to identify this source.
12   "A hundred years" (*Sto lat*) is a Polish song traditionally sung for birthdays, and the phrase "Sto lat!" ("[May you live] a hundred years!") is used in Polish as "Happy birthday!" is used in English.

intention. Twelve sisters are supposed to go there, including Sister A. It will be very emotional for us to be separated, and then we will have to make great efforts to fill this huge void.

I now have a very pleasant task, conducive to meditation (alas, not only the intended and desired kind), as I am embroidering a linen tablecloth with stitches I learned while I was still in Perepelniki—a multicolored folk pattern. I spend hours at it (stitching the pattern). It's restful and prayerful work because it does not require much attention at all. A real blessing; may I not squander it as I often do.

November 22, 1958

The active apostolate is not my task

During the Christmas season, we listened to borrowed records with Father Duval[13] singing beautiful songs about God and playing his guitar, which he performs in cafés and restaurants with great success. I wrote him [her brother] the address of the publishing house that records and distributes these songs, asking him to send me sheet music, since records are terribly expensive . . .

I am becoming more and more convinced that nothing can be done in this matter without prayer and sacrifice, and that certainly the active apostolate (letters, conversations, lending books, etc.) is not my task. And even those who do this in the world will also do nothing if they themselves are not united with God through prayer and sacrifice . . .

I owe this card with the gorgeous Bernadette to Sister N., who, among other earthly possessions, gave up Antoine de Saint-Exupéry's book *Wind, Sand and Stars* for me to send to Aunt Lela for Christmas, which I did. So, of course, I will give her this card with a quote from Saint Louis Grignon de Montfort, the same as on the commemorative card of Father Wojtyła's episcopal consecration: "All yours".

Last week a great external change took place in my life, because I got a single cell to use. Until now I always lived with someone else. That was also very wonderful and sweet, but a cell of solitude is

---

13   Aimé Lucien Duval (1918–1984), better known under the name of Père Duval, was a French Jesuit priest, songwriter, singer, and guitarist, who had great success in the fifties and sixties. Tragically he was an alcoholic and unsuccessfully attempted suicide, after which he promoted awareness of addiction and frequented meetings of Alcoholics Anonymous.

wonderful and actually a perfect state according to the constitutions. So, I am still rejoicing in this blessing.

Besides, my habit, scapular, and under-tunic have been patched. Also, today Forty Hours' Devotion and Exposition of the Most Blessed Sacrament have started. And another joy, that my Sabcia,[14] enchanted with Laski, will most likely settle there. She brought me a piece of Saint Agatha's blessed bread, so that I would never run out of it. She was charmed by the chapel, Father Fedorowicz, and everything "in general."

February 11, 1959

Foundation in Siedlce

Since Wednesday, November 24, Reverend Mother has been in Siedlce, where she went with twelve sisters. On November 29 the first Holy Mass was celebrated in the monastery chapel by Bishop Świrski[15] of Siedlce and Father Piotr. The plasterwork in the monastery has not dried yet, and it is very cold and wet (the bed linens are damp). They have their own central heating, but every now and again something breaks, the pipes burst, and they are flooded. On top of that, they still have no coke[16] for the winter, and they are "hanging on" to Providence (stylishly). Reverend Mother will help them get settled there until December 7th. We get a call from them every other day. The farewell was quite tearful, so that the handkerchiefs were used a lot. Sister A. may have had a dry eye, but I am certain that she cried in private. The day before the ceremony with the Bishop — because there was still the consecration of the cornerstone for the church — when they arrived in a hurry with Reverend Mother, they discovered it was the Augean stable that needed to be cleaned. They worked all day and all night. And some of them had already worked many such days and nights. We have breathed a sigh of relief that they are already there and that they can now settle in peacefully. And the most important thing is that they already have the Blessed Sacrament under their roof as well as daily Mass. It is a great miracle that it all came to be, a great

---

14 Sabina Czerniewska.
15 Servant of God Ignacy Świrski (1885–1968), Bishop of Siedlce from 1946 to 68.
16 A type of fuel with a high carbon content and few impurities, made by heating coal or oil in the absence of air.

wonder, and a great joy for us. Three years of efforts and sacrifices, worries, failures, and troubles. The new stage now is not easy either, but probably not so hard as before.

November 27, 1959

Everything I have done so far is just a fraud

I need to concentrate and not allow myself to be distracted, which I tend to do, and which is my downfall. Of course, if you love God strongly and fervently, nothing can stop you on your way to Him, and otherwise it is easy to find excuses. I owe so much to you, dear Mama, more than to anyone else other than God. Please pray and ask for me to truly love Him. Everything that I have done so far is just a fraud, a tragic joke.

January 25, 1960

A huge "dirty job"

I seriously must convert. And that is a huge "dirty job" requiring all my strength. Please don't worry about anything, but be very happy without a shadow of sadness, because it is really a great honor that God needs something from us, that is, from you, Mama, and from me. Alleluia.

June 22, 1960

Crossed off the list of living and sentient beings

Here is what happened. Miss Chrzanowska came to see Sister Kinga yesterday and said that she had heard from Mrs. R. that you, dear Mama, are in the hospital because of a heart attack . . . . Did it not even occur to N. that prayer matters and that it can strengthen a person in suffering sometimes more effectively than material measures? It is possible that my prayer can do little, but I have a multitude of good and loving sisters who have been concerned about the news as if it were someone very close to them, and their prayers would have supported you for three days already, and not just today, if I had been notified right away! Of course, there is no point in giving a reproach and what I have written is just an initial reaction that could not have been different. They think that a person who has entered a monastery can be crossed off the list of living and sentient beings, and they do not know how wrong they are.

September 25, 1960

He wants from us a very simple thing

I feel like I've forgotten half of what I was going to write. So much is on my mind after a joyful night. First of all, I'd like to send my best wishes to you, dear Mama, for Christmas and New Year. There are a lot of them, but they all come down to a common denominator: to be a Christian in the true meaning of the word. As I was reflecting on what the essential qualities of a Christian actually are, I came up with four, but perhaps I've forgotten something. 1. Looking at the world of people and all things only with the eyes of faith. 2. Universal love flowing out of Christ's Love, embracing everything He loves, and so every man without exception. 3. A certain ease in forgiving all wrongs and insults and not holding grudges against anyone, among other things thanks to the awareness that God has forgiven me a debt infinitely greater than anything I feel like "strangling" my neighbors for, and if I do not forgive them wholeheartedly, God's forgiveness toward me will also be with reservations. 4. Humility, meekness, obedience .... I left out one more trait that is also definitely important, because Saint Paul talks about it all the time: constant joy and serenity in everything [cf. Phil 3 and 4] .... It is better not to assert one's earthly rights by anything. Neither with thought, nor with word, nor with gesture; everything that was, cut it off and throw it "into the depths of the sea," and think only of what is. And the Lord God is. He is in us. And He wants from us a very simple thing: that we may enjoy His current presence and trust in His ideas without any care or anxiety.

December 18, 1960

There is no need to shed tears over our temporary separation

Yesterday, for example, when after serving in the refectory I sat down on a bench in our courtyard and the blackbird on the gutter whistled so wonderfully that I felt you were right next to me, dear Mama, and I thought how wonderful it would be one day in the home of our Heavenly Father, where we will experience the most wonderful concerts and spectacles together in the Most Holy Trinity. That is why there is no need to shed tears over our temporary separations, which are moving us towards a fuller meeting. There is nothing negative in our separation.

April 7, 1961

The road to this heaven can be tiring

The [Council] album was lot of work for me. Three weeks of very hard work plus Christmas, which means a ton of work in the monastery. "In heaven we shall rest."

As far as sleep, things are better in that when I can't fall asleep, I don't get upset like I used to and I accept this situation with resignation, even more...

During the three-day retreat before the renewal of vows on January 1, we listened to four conferences by Father Aleksander Fedorowicz. It was the culmination of everything I have ever heard in my life. It was recorded on a tape recorder. I finished the album on January 4. And that's why I didn't actually have a "normal" retreat, that is, with prayer, but a pretty abnormal one. Perhaps I'll make up for it a bit now. It's already late. Please don't hold it against me that I write rarely and briefly, but this is God's plan. "In heaven we shall rest"; that's good. And that the road to this heaven can be tiring—it's all right and no wonder. But there is something to look forward to, so let's "go walking, whistling."

January 6, 1962

I don't even care anymore that my stitches hurt from laughing

I just wrote a daily message to the Reverend Mother, and since I am still quite weak, I can't afford a second one, so I asked her to give it to you, my first, one-and-only mother. I'm lying around, doing a bit of walking, and I think I'll be home by the middle of Easter week. I am glad that I am "making a good impression" because both the sick and the doctors cannot get over the fact that a nun can be so cheerful. I think that the glory of the Bridegroom grows through this, so I don't even care anymore that my stitches hurt from laughing.

I wish you, my dear parents, a happy Easter, despite everything, and I am sending you my best wishes...

undated letter, written probably April 19, 1963

2

Excerpts from Letters to Her Cousin Danuta Szczepańska

I am getting to know the charism of the order

Danusia, if you only knew how terribly sublime our vocation is! When I came here, I was completely unaware of it. I was only filled with some "great need" that pushed me here two years ago (you remember how it was). Now, as I am getting to know the charism of the Institute,[1] I see more and more that there is nothing for a person to do here, except for one thing: to "incapacitate" oneself completely so that God can do what He wants—which also, of course, could not happen without Him.

You probably know that we are concerned with making amends for offenses and sacrileges, which is possible only in union with the Lord Jesus...

Think about how much grace it takes to fulfill such a vocation, and how pure the love that it requires. And how irrevocably one must trust in the Lord God, so as not to die from fear of one's own misery and weakness. So, pray for us from time to time, for this is in the interests of the Mystical Body.

The thought of you always gives me joy and I "feel" how we are more and more together. It is strange, but real. That is why I can go so long without writing to you. Anyway, you know it yourself.

You have no idea (maybe you do), how I am praying for N. to see how good our God is and how worthy of love. I am sure that he will see that, and will love Him more truly than you and I do.

June 15, 1953

---

[1] For more on the charism of the Institute, see the sources mentioned in the appendix.

It's just play before you know Him enough to never want to leave Him again

You've made me so happy with this photo of Michał, who is delightful and in general adorable beyond words. Oh, Danusia, may you raise them well! And keep them from harm! When I read your last letter, I realized that this must really be the greatest thing for you. And here we shall meet. It's about the question of the Lord God in your soul, and we know from our own experience that it's just play before you know Him enough to never want to leave Him again. It must be, apart from caring, a very effective "spur" to keep nourishing yourself and have something to give them. It seems to me that this is terribly important. The most important and the most difficult. But that which is worthwhile must cost a lot, and when a person refreshes his conviction that supernatural things surpass everything that can be dear in this world, then it is easier to exert yourself and to lose various things, and thus to free yourself and to make yourself independent of that which troubles you from within and without.

So I want to wish you on your name day lots and lots of everything! And perhaps most of all, that which I ask for myself and for which I ask the most, the grace of faith! For when you believe, you worry about nothing, and you have this joy, "for the joy of the Lord is our strength" [Neh 8:10]. And this is the truth and confidence that shatters the greatest obstacles.

Indeed, and I am almost sure of it, pride is the worst thing that can threaten a person in life, and that's the evil that you're so afraid of for your children in their lives. This is it!

Please give my thanks to Anulka for the drawings. I tried to make something equally good today at recreation, but it turned out not to be easy.

June 20, 1954

It's better to get to know the saints from authentic and objective sources

Van der Meersch[2] does not enjoy a good reputation in our community because he supposedly messed things up in a fundamental

---

2   Maxence van der Meersch (1907–1951), author of *La petite Sainte Thérèse* (published in 1943, with a Polish edition in 1954), came from a troubled family of freethinkers. He converted to Catholicism in 1936 and wrote, in addition to novels, two religious biographies: this one about Saint Thérèse, and another on the Curé of Ars.

but very subtle way, so that even priests do not realize that something important is missing. He forgot that holiness in Christ's Church consists in the development of grace in the soul and therefore super-natural life. And he supposedly presented it [holiness] as if it consisted only in man's acknowledgment of his misery and nothingness, which of course is thrilling if one can act consistently according to this truth that one has recognized and acknowledged in oneself. Magnanimity and heroism are required for that, which naturally delights everyone. But the point is that if the author leads the reader to this admiration, which is more an admiration for man than for God in man, and tells him, "See, this is holiness in the Catholic Church" — he threw the baby out with the bathwater! Talk to your priest (Wojtyła) about it, if you wish, and you will have the opportunity to do so: I am curious what he thinks about the book.

It's better to learn about the saints and get to know them from authentic and objective sources, and not from some novelist's ramblings. Certainly, "to them that love God, all things work together unto good" [Rom 8:28], but only to a certain extent. Such errors are the more pernicious the more subtle and hidden they are. Try to reconsider it some more; I urge you to do so. You understand that after what I know of this book, I no longer want to read it or have it, because it does not smell of "the good odor of Christ" [cf. 2 Cor 2:15].

December 27, 1954

This thought fortifies me when I am troubled by my ailments

I would be very grateful if you could drop me a line about whether you have already gotten over your strep throat and in general about how you are doing. I can only help you with prayer, and I am no good at this! I worry at the thought that you are overloaded, because having too much on your plate is not good. I console myself with the fact that, if God allows any evil, it is only so that, with His help, it can be overcome with good [cf. Rom 12:21], which most often means patience. Saint Benedict, in the Prologue to the *Rule*, says that through patience we shall share in the suf-ferings of Christ. You have no idea how this thought fortifies me when I am troubled excessively by my ailments and when, as is my custom, I want to get angry and throw off this "yoke" which, of course, is adding insult to injury. I often think of you as my Sister

Magdalene[3] and that you have this name for a reason . . .

I was unable to talk to N. as I should have, especially since I know from my mother that he had "lost his faith," etc., and the conversation did not flow at all. But "*non loquendo sed moriendo*" (see the Collect from the Feast of the Holy Innocents).[4] Regarding his faith, I think in his case it was like baby teeth: it was never strong, or rather he never held on to it firmly until he finally let it go. I trust that when he gets wiser, he will start looking for it himself until he finds it. Pray about that sometimes, please. A lot depends on it.

July 3, 1956

The point is to give everything one does the proper direction

Time is flying by terribly fast for me, too, and this makes me think and work for eternity much more fiercely than before. I think the point is to give everything one does the proper direction, and thus not to do only this or that, but to fulfill the will of God in all the toiling, which is not lacking in the monastery; and naturalism is so deeply rooted in man. Lately I have been exerting myself from morning till evening, so as not to fall asleep at the most inappropriate moment, in which I resemble a little the Apostles in Gethsemane. Only my sleepiness does not come from sadness but from bile and liver disorders, so don't be sad about it, because it is completely normal after this surgery, and now we have a good doctor who took me under his care. God has arranged it so wonderfully that I can be completely unconcerned about it.

December 26, 1956

How could it not be a waste to give God to man?

It occurred to me during Christmas Day Lauds: how could it not be a waste to give God to man? I feel that this matter will torment me till I die; it cannot be otherwise (this instead of a card for which there was no time).

I imagine that you are awfully busy with your sick and healthy ones, and on that account the Lord God takes care of your soul with no less care; I think it is certainly so. There is always some great peace in doing His will, however strange it may be, isn't there?

January 31, 1957

---

3   Mrs. Szczepańska's name as a Benedictine oblate.
4   "O God, whose praise the martyred Innocents on this day confessed, not by speaking, but by dying . . ."

No gap between church and "ordinary life"

I have been thinking about what you wrote to me about Anulka regarding Holy Communion, etc., and it seems to me that the ideal would be if through the reading of the Gospels, children could befriend the Lord Jesus and through that make both a lifelong and practical connection. You know, so that there's no gap between the church and prayer in general and "ordinary life." Because if they are completely disconnected, then you are just cultivating superficial piety for show.

January 18, 1959

Each year it's been more wonderful, a whole new adventure

I calculated that this is the tenth Christmas I've spent at the monastery, and each year it's been more wonderful, and a whole new adventure. Once, when it was my turn to remain in reparative Adoration, which lasts several hours,[5] I had time to think about how God had actually brought me here. And I noticed, not for the first time, that it pleased Him to give me a lot through you. That's why my wishes for you this year, which I "send" as earnestly and often as I can, have a special tone to them. I am asking God to show you gratitude for me in His own way.

May He empower you to receive all that He wants to give you, and that gift is He Himself. Let us pray for this; you for me, and I for you. In fact, everything boils down to love and therefore nothing prevents a person from living a life of peace and joy with God. This is what I am wishing you with this Christmas wafer,[6] and this is what I want you to wish me, and this is what we should pray for.

December 18, 1960

---

5 The *amende honorable* was a civil punishment that required an offender to be led into a church or square, where, with torch in hand and a rope around his neck, he would beg pardon on his knees for some crime. For her monasteries, Mother Mectilde established a spiritual version of the *amende honorable*, or act of reparation: the designated reparator of the day says a prayer in front of the Blessed Sacrament, kneeling in the middle of the choir, with a lighted candle in hand and having, about the neck, the rope that signifies a humble and penitent solidarity with all poor sinners. The designated reparator usually had a longer watch of adoration than on other days, and it is this to which Sister Bernadette refers.

6 The Christmas wafer (Polish: *opłatek*) is a Catholic Christmas tradition in Poland. Unleavened wafers, embossed with Christmas images, are broken and shared by all participating in a Christmas Eve dinner, and they are often mailed to family or friends who are unable to share the meal. A sign of reconciliation and forgiveness as well as friendship and love, the breaking of *opłatek* is always accompanied by good wishes.

EGO DILECTO MEO, ET AD ME CONVERSIO EJUS

"I to my beloved, and his turning is towards me" (Sg 7:10) is the text which here accompanies a striking combination of symbols. Does the lily represent the virgin brides to whom Christ's presence is communicated by the Cross and the Blessed Sacrament? "And each year it's been more wonderful," Sister Bernadette writes.

We are not smart and good

The Lord God is the only doctor and cure for this. It's just a matter of being in constant contact with Him and receiving it constantly as well. For the past few years, I have been in the process of discovering and unearthing this truth from the rubble of self-love, the many floors of which are still standing, that it is not I in myself who should be good, etc., but He and He alone in me. Every discovery and experience leads to this: that He may be everything and may free us from this stupid anguish; that we are not smart and good, but we are nothing, and the center of gravity shifts more and more from our own selves to the Lord Jesus. Perhaps your path is also similar, because you are my cousin, or perhaps not?

April 7,1961

Pray for me that I don't squander my vocation on trifles

Things are going well for me, even very well. Of course, we are still in a state of war,[7] but this is war during peacetime. Time flies by and the whole point is not to lose it and to string every moment and matter onto the thread of divine vision and will. Pray for me sometimes that I don't squander my vocation on trifles, because it's awfully easy in a strange life like ours, where everything is rooted in faith. And now I am healthy, you know? A relatively new state for me and still very precious. Maybe I owe it to those who are sick? In the Mystical Body such exchanges can take place . . .

I wish you for Christmas and the New Year a union with God in faith, hope, and love, and a living contact with Him in constant prayer.

December 17, 1961

---

7   Poland was not at war with anyone at that time, and martial law (a possible translation of the Polish phrase "*stan wojenny*" used in the original) was not declared until 1981, so this must be a reference to spiritual warfare.

Sister Bernadette's illumination of
Saint Benedict in the Evangeliarium.

3
Excerpts from letters to Sister Augustina Zakrzewska

I am often "glad we do not have to try to kill the stars"

It would be good if you could already arrive[1]; that is what I want to tell you above all, Sister.

Besides that, there was a storm at night, and now the sky is bluer than it was on July 20.

I am reading the book for the second time.[2] I have befriended it as much as you can befriend a book. I can't explain how close it all is to me, and how helpful in catching my fish. Because I, too, am often "glad we do not have to try to kill the stars."

August 3, 1958, monthly retreat

The very act of seeking brings life

I think of you often, Sister, especially when I come across something in the Psalms, or when I look at the flowers in the black pot in the choir.

Psalm 68 has a verse that reads: *Quaerite Deum et vivet anima vestra* [68:33].[3] It is not just when you find Him that your soul comes alive, but the very act of seeking the Living God brings it to life. And in the Epistle to the Corinthians we read, "God hath called us in peace" [1 Cor 7:15].

And the third "pearl" that I cherish and nurture is the first of the eight beatitudes, which recurs in different forms throughout the Psalms, almost in each one of them. I keep discovering more and more that "there is something to them"...

September 27, 1958

---

1   The first few letters anticipate Sister Augustina's entry into the monastery.
2   Namely, Ernest Hemingway, *The Old Man and the Sea.*
3   Seek ye God, and your soul shall live.

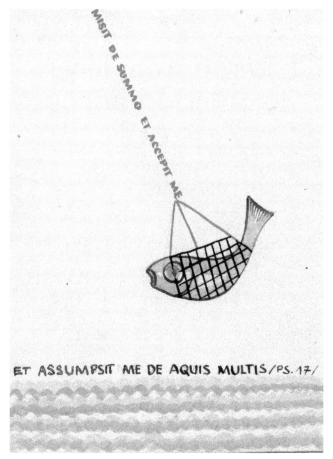

Sister Bernadette's love and knowledge of the Psalms finds a humorous expression in her depiction of a verse from Psalm 17: "He sent from on high, and took me: and received me out of many waters."

Sister, just leave everything behind and come!

I would love to write back to you, but the waiting room is not conducive, and in a few hours I will be going into retreat for ten days.

SISTER! Sister, just leave everything behind and come! There is no other way—I am telling you, Sister. Just think: if you were paralyzed, for example, the professor would say: "Poor thing!" and would have to reconcile himself to the situation. If you died, he would be very upset about it and, out of necessity, he would find someone to take your place. If some man, the one and only, crossed your path, and you had a chance to fly with him to some lands of happiness even today, the professor would have to step aside and even congratulate you, and escort you to the airport with a tear in his eye.

Meanwhile, the reason for this loss is *infinitely* more important, because the Lord Jesus Himself is waiting for you. Letting someone down is inevitable, and certainly it is better to let down all creatures

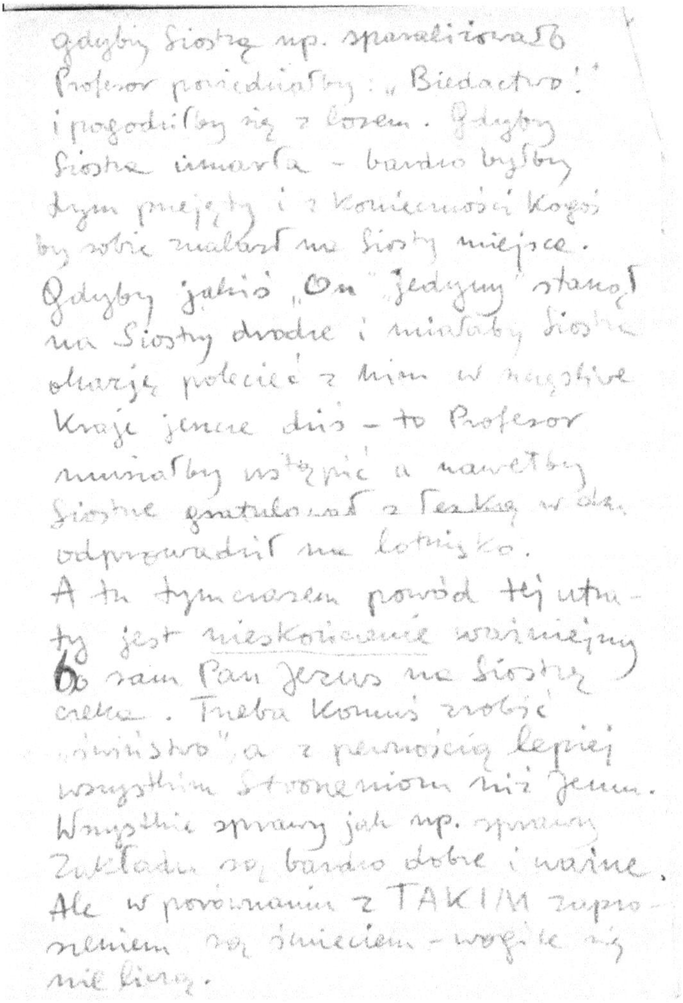
Gdyby Siostrę np. sparaliżowało
Profesor powiedziałby: „Biedactwo!"
i pogodziłby się z losem. Gdyby
Siostra umarła – bardzo byłby
tym przejęty i z konieczności ktoś
by sobie znalazł na Siostry miejsce.
Gdyby jakiś „On" „Jedyny" stanął
na Siostry drodze i miałaby Siostra
okazję polecieć z nim w szczęśliwe
kraje jeszcze dziś – to Profesor
musiałby ustąpić a nawet by
Siostrze gratulował z łezką w oku,
odprowadził na lotnisko.
A tu tymczasem powód tej utra-
ty jest nieskończenie ważniejszy
bo sam Pan Jezus na Siostrę
czeka. Trzeba komuś zrobić
„świństwo" a z pewnością lepiej
wszystkim stworzeniom niż Jemu.
Wszystkie sprawy jak np. sprawy
Zakładu są bardzo dobre i ważne.
Ale w porównaniu z TAKIM zapro-
szeniem są śmieciem – wcale się
nie liczą.

"But compared to THIS invitation they are garbage—they count for nothing at all," is the phrase visible at the bottom of this page of Sister Bernadette's moving letter of October 16, 1958.

than to disappoint Him. All matters, such as the affairs of the Institute, are very good and important. But compared to THIS invitation they are garbage — they count for nothing at all.

You have to expose yourself to some measure of unpleasantness, and this from those whom you value and respect very much. Blood must be shed, and you can't say goodbye to this world in such an "elegant" way. But the "buzz" will be short-lived and the position you left will be filled sooner than it seems.

It seems to me as if (emotionally) the two sides of the scales are balanced in your case:

1) contemplative life

2) apostolic life in the world, with and for people.

For you can be a candle and enjoy your "own" flame, watching and enjoying the scattered darkness and the warmth that radiates around it, but you can also be a lump of coal thrown into a giant furnace that heats the whole world, whose only task is to burn out completely and see nothing but God in whom and for whom are all things [cf. Rom 11:36]... Now I'm home, and I think all that I've written is very rough, and I guess it has to stay that way, because I just don't have the time or the glossy paper anymore.

I am sending you hugs with all my might and wish you, as always: P. D. S. S. N. [4]

October 16, 1958

I rejoice at the thought of encounters on the paths in paradise

I was wondering today in the choir (Thursday Exposition) if you go to the Felician Sisters on Smoleńsk Street; they always have Exposition there. I would be happy if you could go there so that your adoration could start already... I used to sneak out there often before I entered, and it was very good. That's something I dream of for you, that you could spend a lot of time there. Because this is most precious in life, these moments with God. I also think that in heaven the "Communion of Saints" will be important, and I rejoice at the thought of this and that meeting on the paths of paradise. But here much must be lost and cast away, or rather must

---

4   *Pax Domini Sit Semper Nobiscum,* "May the peace of the Lord be always with us."

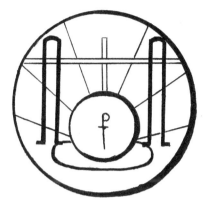

HOC EST ENIM
CORPUS MEUM

Another line drawing from The Mass of a Soul. Sister Bernadette writes,
"Through grace we already have the essence of paradise here — the Lord God."

be postponed for later, that is, for paradise. Through grace we already have the essence of paradise here — the Lord God.

November 27, 1958

But I did not forsake myself — how abominable!

When I think back and remember my past experiences similar to this, I blush with shame that I was able to forsake "everything" and MOTHER, but I did not forsake myself — how abominable! I beg you now to do this for me and for yourself, so that I may be converted through your sacrifice.

You need to be able to keep your cool when you witness your own wretchedness!

January 25, 1959

I guess the monastery is that very donation box

It is difficult for me to express what I would like to say to you, which fills me up and which I want to share with you. I don't know if you've read about the Holy Father's proposed Ecumenical Council which he wants to convene at the end of this year to unite Protestants and schismatics with the Catholic Church.[5] This was read to

---

5   When the Second Vatican Council was convened, it was initially perceived as a council for the reunification of Christians.

us at lunch time. I don't know if there is anything that would be a greater torment to the Lord Jesus than this tearing apart of His Body, which has been going on for so many centuries and which is such an obstacle to the expansion of His Kingdom. And by the same token, perhaps most of all things, His Heart is concerned with healing His Bride from this horrible affliction. Pascal said that Christ will be in agony on the Cross until the end of the world, and in light of this, His "I thirst" [Jn 19:28] still endures.[6]

Sister!!! I sense deeply that we are enmeshed in this whole story, that we are the ones at stake here, and that it is up to us to decide how it unravels, on the simple principle that we are members of one body. Sister! If there was a box set aside for donations to this cause, we should all jump into that box. I guess the monastery is that very box, and it is a great joy that as long as we are alive, we can continue to renew this offering at almost every step. It doesn't matter that sometimes it's "damp," but the Lord Jesus knows that we should not worry about that.

February 13, 1959

I assure you it is practical!

Sister! I have found that the most practical way to give yourself to God is as if you were to give someone a thing and never ask for it back. You will have peace of mind!

God seems to like it very much when we burden Him with such troubles, so that we can be at ease.

Would you subscribe to that theory? I assure you it is practical! Please nod your head to me (or don't) when you have a chance. *DN*.[7]

March 2, 1959

The devil is doing his best to fuel our anxieties

Sister! God bless you for your "letter" and self-portrait. During that recreation I somehow could not concentrate and reply to you. I am glad that you like it that way. Because if you have such a thought as the foundation, then at times of upheaval you

---

6   Pascal, "The Mystery of Jesus": "Jesus will be in agony until the end of the world. We must not sleep during that time." In *Pensées*, ed. and trans. Roger Ariew (Indianapolis, IN: Hackett, 2004), S749/L919, p. 273.

7   *Dominus nobiscum*, "May the Lord be with us."

can easily and quickly regain your equilibrium. And that is the value of the foundation — not in promising yourself consistency and fretting over the fact that there are deviations. It is just as meaningless as promising "that I will do better." I have come to understand that one can only promise and resolve to strive earnestly for improvement, but that improvement itself is the work of the Lord God, for which He waits until a person is perfectly humble. They say that self-love dies fifteen minutes after a person's death,[8] so, "no word shall be impossible with God" [Lk 1:37], and thus we rejoice in hope [cf. Rom 12:12] because "how much more will your Father from heaven give the good Spirit to them that ask him?" [Lk 11:13], and, "thou hast not forsaken them that seek thee, O Lord" [Ps 9:11]. Nothing can be more certain. The devil is doing his best to derail us and fuel our anxieties, and he is glad when he manages to cast us into sadness and despondency. Let us not give him this pleasure. DN.

February–March, 1959, 11:30pm, I cannot fall asleep.

I understood how many things need to be "deleted"

Thank you, Sister!!! I strive to constantly thank the Lord God for all the good that He continually pours upon us. What a blessing that we are to be of "Perpetual Adoration" — because if we are already called that, it is not an exaggeration to really strive for that perpetuity.

I have not been sweating any more since yesterday and can pray and think a little more. And that's what keeps running through my mind, that time is short, because you don't know at what watch the Lord will come [cf. Lk 12:38], so dimly lit is the lamp [cf. Mt 25:1–13]. Such is the practical conclusion I draw from these meditations, to constantly "delete as applicable." During those few days of lying down, probably thanks to your prayers, I understood how many things there are to be deleted and how much valuable space is gained by doing so. I am very, very grateful to you. I try to pray "for the postulants."

March 1959

---

8   A well-known saying of Saint Francis de Sales.

4
Excerpts from Letters to a College Friend, Ewa Szczęk[1]

If a man is good and worthy of great love, what about God?
Don't worry, because the fact that your thoughts are scattered doesn't mean that you can't pray. THE WILL: that is the crux of the matter. If I want to pray because it is the will of God, and if I spend these five minutes only rejecting external thoughts and returning constantly to the Presence of God, "this prayer pierces the heavens"..., although I feel nothing but this dull struggle. For this is the true state of things. Man can do nothing by his own strength, but it is through persistent prayer, initially just like that one—actually, not much of a prayer, barren and difficult prayer—that the Lord God begins to show man his total dependence on Himself, so that gradually prayer becomes the breath of the soul. It is only through persistent prayer that more and more wonderful horizons, happiness and joy, open before the eyes of the soul, to which nothing in the world can be compared, just as the Creator and the creation cannot be compared. If the view from Babia Góra then—do you remember?—if that view from Babia Góra was so breathtaking, then what can we say about the One who created it from nothing? Or, if a man is good and worthy of great love, what about God, who is Goodness and Love itself? It is enough to look at the Cross to see where that love led Him, or at the Host. He knew that He would be trampled upon, but nevertheless He stayed.

January 16, 1956

---

1   Married name: Czarnocka-Januszkowska.

If the Lord God is everything, why should I be anything?

I know and I recognize this "flavor" of limitation, dullness, and coldness of heart; it is all bitter, but it does not belong to the essence of things. What matters is good will, the will directed at seeking and fulfilling the will of God. Beyond that, nothing else depends on man.

I don't know if this will comfort you, because as for me, I have found a way not to worry about my own wretchedness, limitation, and lowliness, because if the Lord God is everything, why should I be anything? Since I have made this discovery, I have enjoyed great happiness because the great weight of various worries has fallen away. For instance, when some humiliation or adversity occurs, I think to myself, "How fortunate that I am nothing, because if I were something, I would have to worry and spend a long time 'massaging the afflicted spot.'"

Pysio's words about mountaineering are profound and touchingly close. Personally, I consider mountaineering to be the noblest sport on account of its pure selflessness and because of that primacy of spirit not found in other sports. But precisely because it is so sublime, it requires from a man what he lacks so much in moments of victory — deep humility.

Besides, there seems to be no human enterprise that should be excluded from the current of man's ultimate purpose, as if on the margins of his supernatural destiny (the Holy Father, when he recently received athletes, blessed their equipment). How often I think of climbing, which turns out so well to be that essential "climb" to union with God; there are so many analogies! For example, the first moment of the descent, when you have to leave the rock, and entrust yourself to the rope. It's very similar when one has to leave the human way of seeing and descend into the dark abyss on a rope, which is unconditional faith. The only difference is that here the security and certainty is absolute despite the fear, while there it is only relative. There are many similarities every step of the way. You know, then, that man's goal so infinitely surpasses his wildest dreams and that every moment of this life is a step on the way to that goal, so everything in this world that has any connection with man must be purposeful with a capital P.

October 26, 1956

There is no sorrow that could not be soothed and transformed by His birth

On Christmas Eve I will be with you more than usual with all my heart and prayers. The joy and peace that the Lord Jesus brings us by His coming and Redemption are of divine proportions, and therefore there is no sorrow in the world that could not be soothed and transformed by His birth, and no tears that would not cease and change from bitter to sweet at the sight of His weeping. I will pray earnestly for all these graces and God's assistance for you . . . . For since God became Man, man has ceased to be alone in carrying the suffering, and henceforth it has ceased to be pointless. In fact, everything that has a purpose is no longer evil. With this Christmas wafer [*opłatek*], I send you my wishes for this Christmas and the New Year. Our power is in God and not in us, and the burdens that weigh us down will become light if we confidently and continually ask for help in all our thoughts and affairs. For these burdens are calculated for this twofold capacity. If the most important capacity, God, is lacking, we will break down.

December 16, 1956

Prayer can last three seconds

When I read about people who have made such a great use of this life, it makes me want to make sure I don't waste mine, because it's possible in a monastery, too. And I always think of you. Because, you know, the purpose of life is love — there is no question about that. But love is a great and difficult thing, because it requires self-renunciation and the denial of one's own self. The greater the love, the less the difficulty. You have probably experienced this in marriage. I am sure that if you love, you will feel that you are on the right path and you will be happy, and if you give yourself out of love, you will be very happy. That is why I pray that you will love God, who out of love became Man and who took His love as far as death on the Cross and as far as becoming nourishment for us. There is no greater cause in the world than His cause. His holy Resurrection guarantees to us that there is no risk in giving our lives to someone who is "the Resurrection and the Life" [cf. Jn 11:25]. To be moved by these great truths of faith and to be moved to action, one needs the grace freely given by God. And to receive grace from God, one must ask for it humbly, but briefly and simply, trustingly and persistently, and that is prayer. It can last three seconds, in a tram or in the street. The Lord Jesus in the Gospel said that if man, though evil, gives bread rather than a stone to the child who asks, then will not God, from whom all fatherhood comes, give a good spirit to those who ask Him day and night [cf. Eph 3:15; Lk 11:11–13]. These and many other passages from the Gospel sever the head of all temptations, most notably those against trusting in God's goodness. The Gospel shows us what the Lord God is like, how human He is. The Lord Jesus said, "he that seeth me seeth the Father also" [Jn 14:9]. That is why it is so important to look to Him in the Gospel and then it becomes so easy to kneel down and tell Him that you believe in Him and that you love Him . . . . Try it!!! I beg you!!! I beg you to say something to God every day from the bottom of your heart, even if it's just two words, or merely a glance.

April 24, 1957

My extreme stupidity has manifested itself

I think of you very often, and in those thoughts we probably meet a lot. I have a great favor to ask of you!!! That you don't worry even a little bit about not writing to me, because I understand perfectly well that you may have a loathing for writing, and, what's worse, I also understand that my extreme stupidity, which manifested itself in my recent letters to you through me being pushy and impatient, and the imposition of some of my "opinions," may have been an additional suffering for you. I realize now that everything I have written to you confirms the wise proverb that "the satisfied understand not the pain of the starving," and so I am beginning to understand that you must go through everything you are going through, and that it cannot be any different. Because love for the insignificant human person is too great and God alone can reach into these depths. These are His regions, because everything that is love comes from Him and you have to leave it to Him.

July 13, 1958

5
Excerpts from Letters to Various People

Even if your salary went up five times, and you had charm and success, and I don't know what else!

I wish you this Christmas and in general all that I wish for myself, that is, a living faith and the ensuing joy, which nothing can disturb, because it is rooted in the Lord God. In this lies its superiority over other "joys," that it gives man a true autonomy from all the misfortunes and sorrows of life, against which man is powerless without it.

It bothers me that here, in the monastery, by God's marvelous mercy I am as if "at the very bosom" of the Church and of Grace, while you are suffering tribulations there ... But these are only emotional grumblings, because in fact, I am certain that in every place, the Lord God keeps ready what He wants to give to everyone; all we need to do is open our mouth. And this is what I wish for you, to open your mouth as wide as possible. "Open thy mouth wide, and I will fill it" (80[:11]). I'm sure Mama has the Psalms, so you can look up this Psalm and see how pretty it is. Have you read this article by Merton[1] in issue 31 of *Znak*[2] entitled "Seeds of Contemplation"? If you haven't, don't be discouraged by the title or the fact that it is a bit heavy, and be sure to read it! That's why I recommend it to you so much, and if you read it carefully, you can really benefit a lot in terms of practical tips.

Monday, the 15th. On the Saturday before Palm Sunday, Joanna came to see me. Before I entered the conversation room, I was sure it would be you, and I was excited to see you, for I had already seen everyone else through the grille, except for you. But I console

---

1   Thomas Merton (1915–1968) was an American Trappist monk and author of over 50 books on monasticism, theology, social justice, and Eastern religion.
2   *Znak*, January 1952. A Polish monthly magazine dedicated to social, cultural, religious, and philosophical topics. It was started in Cracow in 1946 by a group of Catholic intellectuals.

myself that this is entirely unimportant, and that actually such visits do not deepen spiritual ties, and those are the only ones that have value. The fact that I have not seen you for such a long time has not distanced me from you at all, and in some ways you are even closer to me than before, as are all my siblings. I do not know if you understand this, but it really is so.

Tuesday the 16th. How wonderful that it is spring and Easter. In the monastery, or rather in the Church, Easter lasts until the feast of the Ascension. You have no idea how wonderful that is! Because in the world this wonderful holiday ends with the last cake and with a sad sigh that "everything in this world ends," which is not true, because instead everything is just beginning in this world. And that's why after the Feast of the Ascension it's also wonderful, although it's quite different. I'm telling you, if you are ever sad and miserable in the world, it is only because you simply have not yet come to the Church for your daily bread, to which you are entitled as a baptized soul and without which you cannot live or find joy, even if you have time and peace, and even if your salary went up five times at the office, and if you had charm and success, and I don't know what else — all this will exude emptiness, and underneath all this a great privation is lurking. If I hadn't experienced it myself, I wouldn't have been able to tell you. But now I know and that is why I am telling you, because I love you. And I implore you not to get married too hastily, because it really is a terribly serious decision. I, too, am in an analogous situation to you, and I will be taking my perpetual vows in four years at best. Think about it.

To her sister Anna Wolska, later Dąbrowska, April 16, 1952

Silence is closer to the truth than many words

It must have been two years or longer since I last wrote to you, but I think you can sense that this was not an indication of any estrangement between us. Silence has a deeper meaning and is closer to the truth than many words. Because it is closer to the truth, it is closer to God. That is why, for example, our life in the monastery is filled with silence. As silence embraces us and the dust raised by our own noisy selves settles, life begins to show its true colors, free of illusions, and fills us with joy and optimism, because it finally delivers us from the fatal mistake of relying on ourselves for anything. If it were not for this solid foundation in God, in His grace and mercy, all religious vows or even baptismal promises would be completely void, because man himself cannot do anything that would have any value in the supernatural order. My dear old Marcin! I think that when you take all this into account, you will not be frightened that I am not backing down from taking my perpetual vows, especially since the initiative and the first step were not mine. You know me too well to assume that.

I am begging you, please pray for me, because I need so much help before such a great moment. Please pray that in all of this I may fulfill what depends on me, both in preparing for these vows and, above all, for the time after they have been taken. For, although without the help of grace man is not able to take a single step, yet his cooperation with it to a great extent depends on his free will and his free choice. Here man has great dignity and power over his destiny, and the Lord God Himself respects this in man. So let us pray for each other, that our wills may be united with His will, and through this, that our lives may follow the right direction, and that we may always be full of the joy of truth. You know, I have become convinced that the Christian life is worth living.

To her brother, Marcin Wolski, November 6, 1955

As I was learning to sing the antiphons . . .

Today, as I was learning to sing the antiphons for tomorrow's feast of the Apostles Philip and James, I was struck by the words of the Lord Jesus to Saint Philip, "He that seeth me seeth the Father also" (Jn 14[:9]]. The Lord Jesus is the revelation of God to man.

When we attempt to think of God, we tend to be overwhelmed and intimidated by the grandeur of His Majesty, which deters and discourages us. He is so far above us in a realm beyond our reach that we cannot grasp the way He interacts with creation. But instead, we can freely gaze upon the Lord Jesus, for He is God who has revealed Himself to us.

If we want to plunge ourselves into the sanctuary of the mysteries of God our Father—He makes it easy for us, because He tells us how to do it, "This is my beloved son; hear ye him" [Mk 9:6]. This is the solution to everything. Jesus, the helpless infant — that is God. Jesus sitting at the table with sinners and tax collectors — that is God; Jesus weeping over the tomb of Lazarus — that is God; Jesus giving us his Body and Blood — that is God. If we want to know God, let us look at the Lord Jesus, He is the true God. And gazing upon Him, it will not be difficult for us to understand that God is love [cf. 1 Jn 4:16], and only love is our happiness.

To her brother Krzysztof Wolski, April 30, 1956[3]

A nun is also a human being

A nun is also a human being who, despite being externally separated from the world, will never cease to be a daughter and a sister. The fourth commandment is always binding. If one thinks, "The double grille has the effect of cooling the hearts that hide behind it," he is gravely mistaken .... However, I realize and am not surprised that people do not understand such confinement and that it has a chilling effect on them. It is, however, a great divine grace not only to enter a monastery yourself, but also to understand such a decision by someone else.

To her aunt Zofia Kern, December 25, 1956

Everything in our lives that does not point directly to Him is a loss

Thank you, Auntie, for remembering me, praying for me, and sending me your wishes and the Christmas wafer. I also remembered you as I always do, but I do it "silently." I have learned with my own flesh, or rather soul, that the strict regulations which limit our contacts with the "world," that is, even with the closest people, are neither too strict nor excessive. God is indeed such an "inexhaustible" God that everything in our lives that does not point directly to Him is a loss. But surely the Love with which our short and infrequent letters are seasoned is not a loss.

To her aunt Zofia Kern, December 28, 1958

---

3   In the original Polish, the letter is dated April 3, but this is a typo. As the letter indicates, Sister Bernadette's monastery was still observing the feast of Saints Philip and James on its traditional date of May 1, so she would have written this letter on April 30. The feast of Saint Joseph the Worker on May 1, only announced in 1955, was not yet reflected in all liturgical books and ordos.

I am simply a "walking demand" of His mercy

The only consolation I find on your subject is the Scriptures, especially the Psalms, which don't say anywhere that the Lord God is the helper of the happy and the secure, but on the contrary, *Tibi derelictus est pauper, orphano tu eris adiutor* [Ps 9:35][4]. . . . Often, as I come across similar phrases, I think of you and take God at His word. For example, yesterday I found one which reads, "The Lord is good and giveth strength in the day of trouble: and knoweth them that hope in him" [Nah 1:7]. This "knoweth" is wonderful.

I will be very grateful if you would occasionally mention me to the Lord God, because I am simply a "walking demand" of His mercy, which, incidentally, is the very essence of my happiness.

To Zofia Schroederowa, June 2, 1959

I have a weak head and must confine myself to the one thing necessary

My current motto is *carpe diem* [seize the day], so I won't write too much and will run straight to the choir (chapel), taking advantage of Sunday. I am glad that the Christmas wafer came on time and intact; I did not expect such a flattering "review"! Fortunately, I don't have to deal with some of my own artwork "every day," because as soon as I start, I get so passionate and absorbed that all other matters are immediately forgotten. That is why it is very seldom that such a task would be given to me. I have a weak head and must confine myself to the *unum necessarium*.[5]

P. S. Auntie!!! The most important thing! Be sure to read Father Philipon's *La doctrine spirituelle de soeur Elisabeth de la Sainte Trinité* [Paris, 1954]. This should make you happy effectively and permanently, because this is the only thing that may be lacking for happiness. Perhaps I'm thinking like an ant-eater, praising ants to everyone. I will pray a lot and it will be as God wishes, but perhaps you will manage to get a hold of this book and "taste it."

To her aunt Beata Obertyńska, January 15, 1961

I wish you knew what that twenty-year separation was like

Thank you very much, Papa, for the written word, which, in view of your "graphophobia" up to now, is all the more precious to me. I'm

---

4   To thee is the poor man left: thou wilt be a helper to the orphan.
5   The one thing necessary (cf. Lk 10:42).

glad that you have good memories of your stay in our monastery. From the perspective of time, everything that is unpleasant fades in the memory more than that which is pleasant; how fortunate that it is so.

And in the meantime, I was very concerned about you and Mama because of the harsh frosts, to which you are not accustomed and which Mama cannot stand. But apparently it was bearable, since there is no mention of it in your letters.

Thank you for the description of all the lovely details of Christmas at Floriańska, thanks to which I could imagine everything.

The thought of you, Papa, being with Mama gives me great joy and relief as often as I recall it. I wish you knew what that twenty-year separation was like for me! So, it gives me great joy to think that at least at the end of my life I have the comfort of finally having you back. I pray that God will help you by His grace so that your return will be complete and that it can be a source of great joy for you as well. Thanks to God's mercy, as long as man lives, he can always start living anew, even if he has only one hour of life left. And what particularly delights me is that thanks to God's almighty mercy, all the tails of the past dragging behind a man, which disturb and torment him, fall off like a lizard's and the grey-haired man really becomes like a child . . .

I pray that you may have great joy and peace in your soul, Papa, which can only be purchased in the heavenly stores, of course, at the price of some sacrifice, because everything good has to come at a cost.

To her father Kazimierz Wolski, February 2, 1963

FROM HER NOTEBOOK
"Living with the Gospel"

God's Love

"Render therefore . . . to God, the things that are God's." (Mt 22:21)

"He answering, said: Thou shalt love the Lord thy God with thy whole heart, and with thy whole soul, and with all thy strength, and with all thy mind: and thy neighbor as thyself." (Lk 10:27)

"I am come to cast fire on the earth; and what will I, but that it be kindled?" (Lk 12:49)

"God is a spirit; and they that adore him, must adore him in spirit and in truth." (Jn 4:24)

"Abide in me, and I in you." (Jn 15:4)

"I am the vine: you the branches." (Jn 15:5)

"Abide in my love. If you keep my commandments, you shall abide in my love." (Jn 15:9–10)

1. Willing the good of God: "If you loved me, you would indeed be glad, because I go to the Father." (Jn 14:28)
2. Being obedient to God: "If you love me, keep my commandments." (Jn 14:15)
3. Imitating God: "Simon son of John, lovest thou me more than these?" (Jn 21:15) "Follow me." (Jn 21:19)
4. Prayer: "Mary hath chosen the best part" (Lk 10:42), "she hath loved much." (Lk 7:47)
5. Sacrifice — suffering. *Maiorem caritatem nemo habet, ut animam suam ponat quis pro amicis suis.* (Jn 15:13)[1]

"But that the world may know, that I love the Father: and as the Father hath given me commandment, so do I: Arise, let us go hence." (Jn 14:31)

"If you keep my commandments, you shall abide in my love; as I also have kept my Father's commandments, and do abide in his love." (Jn 15:10)

---

1   Greater love than this no man hath, that a man lay down his life for his friends.

"I lay down my life . . . . This commandment have I received of my
Father." (Jn 10: 17–18)

"I live by the Father" (Jn 6:58), "I am in the Father, and the Father
in me." (Jn 14:10)

"I and the Father are one." (Jn 10:30)

Continuous presence

"I will not leave you orphans." (Jn 14:18)

"I am with you all days, even to the consummation of the world."
(Mt 28:20)

1. In Holy Scripture: "Search the scriptures" (Jn 5:39), "Blessed are
they who hear the word of God." (Lk 11:28)
2. In people: "As long as you did it to one of these my least brethren,
you did it to me." (Mt 25:40)
3. In the souls of the just: "If any one love me, he will keep my word,
and my Father will love him, and we will come to him, and will
make our abode with him." (Jn 14:23)
4. In Church authorities: "He that heareth you, heareth me." (Lk 10:16)
5. In the Holy Eucharist: "This is my body." (Mk 14:22)

Sacrifice. Detachment, penance, humility, and the Cross.

"Blessed are the poor in spirit." (Mt 5:3)

"Blessed are they that . . . thirst." (Mt 5:6)

"Blessed are they that mourn." (Mt 5:5)

"Blessed are they that suffer persecution for justice' sake." (Mt 5:10)

"Enter ye in at the narrow gate." (Mt 7:13)

"But this kind is not cast out but by prayer and fasting." (Mt 17:20)

"The kingdom of heaven suffereth violence, and the violent bear it
away." (Mt 11:12)

"If any man will come after me, let him deny himself, and take up
his cross daily, and follow me." (Lk 9:23)

"If any man come to me, and hate not his father, and mother, and
wife, and children, and brethren, and sisters, yea and his own life
also, he cannot be my disciple." (Lk 14:26)

"Every one of you that doth not renounce all that he possesseth,
cannot be my disciple." (Lk 14:23)

"He that loveth his life shall lose it; and he that hateth his life in
this world, keepeth it unto life eternal." (Jn 12:25)

"Unless the grain of wheat falling into the ground die, itself remaineth alone. But if it die, it bringeth forth much fruit." (Jn 12:24–25)

"I, if I be lifted up from the earth, will draw all things to myself." (Jn 12:32)

"When you shall have lifted up the Son of man, then shall you know, that I am he." (Jn 8:28)

"Therefore doth the Father love me: because I lay down my life." (Jn 10:17)

"Greater love than this no man hath, that a man lay down his life for his friends." (Jn 15:13)

"And after eight days were accomplished, that the child should be circumcised." (Lk 2:21)

"Herod will seek the child to destroy him." (Mt 2:13)

"Is not this the carpenter, the son of Mary?" (Mk 6:3)

"He went out into a mountain to pray, and he passed the whole night in the prayer of God." (Lk 6:12)

"And Jesus went about all the cities, and towns, teaching in their synagogues, and preaching the gospel of the kingdom." (Mt 9:35)

"Jesus therefore being wearied with his journey, sat thus on the well. It was about the sixth hour." (Jn 4:6)

"Lying in wait for him." (Lk 11:54)

"They were persecuting him and wanted to kill him." (paraphrase of Lk 22:2 [?])

"Neither did his brethren believe in him." (Jn 7:5)

"Do not we say well that thou ... hast a devil?" (Jn 8:48)

"They took up stones therefore to cast at him." (Jn 8:59)

"They sought therefore to take him." (Jn 10:39)

"He wept over it." (Lk 19:41)

"My soul is sorrowful even unto death." (Mt 26:38)

"He began to grow sorrowful and to be sad." (Mt 26:37)

"And his sweat became as drops of blood, trickling down upon the ground." (Lk 22:44)

"[They] took Jesus, and bound him." (Jn 18:12)

"One of the servants standing by, gave Jesus a blow." (Jn 18:22)

"And some began to spit on him, and to cover his face, and to buffet him ..., and the servants struck him with the palms of their hands." (Mk 14:65)

"Crucify him, crucify him." (Jn 19:6)

"Then therefore, Pilate took Jesus, and scourged him." (Jn 19:1)

"And platting a crown of thorns, they put it upon him.... And they struck his head with a reed: and they did spit on him." (Mk 15:17, 19)

"And bearing his own cross, he went forth to that place which is called Calvary, but in Hebrew Golgotha." (Jn 19:17)

"And they gave him to drink wine mingled with myrrh; but he took it not." (Mk 15:23)

"They crucified him." (Jn 19:18)

"And they that passed by, blasphemed him." (Mt 27:39)

"My God, my God, why hast thou forsaken me?" (Mt 27:46)

"And bowing his head, he gave up the ghost." (Jn 19:30)

E W A N G E L I A .

M ó j Boże, wszystkie słowa
pochodzą od Ciebie. Przygotowałeś
te głosy i otworzyłeś serca.
Jesteś Słowo jedyne i żyjące,
zawierające wszystko, oświetlając
i dające życie wszystkiemu
innemu. Ewangelia ofiarowuje
memu sercu bogatą substancję
Twego Słowa, jego samego. Słyszę
Ciebie, widzę i odkrywam na
każdej stronie, w każdej linijce,

w każdym słowie oblicze Tego, którego jedynie chcę
poznać, kochać, naśladować. Ewangelia, to już jest Eu-
charystia: Ty siebie dajesz i czynisz się naszym
duchowym pokarmem. Słowa są zasłoną pod którą się
ukrywasz. Lecz to jest dobrze, że my czytając je z wiarą przekraczamy powierzchnię. Ty jesteś rozkosznym
owocem okrywanym przez nie i chcę się nimi żywić
i w tej godzinie przychodzę przykarmić się Twoim
świętym Ciałem.

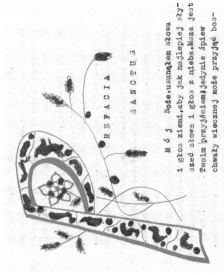

R E P A R A C I A

S A N C T U S

M ó j Boże, usunąłem słowa
i głos ziemi, aby jak najlepiej słyszeć słowa i głos z nieba. Msza jest
Twoim przyjściem; jedynie śpiew
chwały wiecznej może przyjąć bos-

kiego Króla, którego wielbi zawsze.
O boski Królu, nie przychodzisz bez Twojego
dworu. Dzięki jakiej tajemnicy towarzyszy Ci anioł
Rowie i święci? Nie szukam wyjaśnienia. Wiem, że tak
jest, nie może być inaczej. Miłość nie może być bez
swoich miłośników. Oto głos, który chcę słyszeć i z
którym chcę zjednoczyć swój głos; Aniołowie i Archa-
niołowie, Trony i Panowania, Księstwa i Potęgi, Che-
rubini i Serafini. Wy, którzy jesteście więksi nad
wszystkie duchy i blaskiem i wielkością a mimo to
jesteście dla mnie prawdziwymi przyjaciółmi i brać-
mi..

DIGNUS

SUM

NON

DOMINE

CONSECRACIO

O to Jezu, święty moment par excellence, boski moment gdy przychodzisz do nas.

Ale jak Ty przychodzisz?Co wtedy dzieje się na ołtarzu?zaledwie ośmielam się o tym myśleć .To jest tak dziwne i tak wielkie tę nagła przemiana chleba i wina w Twoje Ciało i Twoją Krew,ta realna obec- ność Twojej nieskończonej Piękności pod pozorem benalnej substancji materialnej tak pospolitej ... i ta tajemnicza całopalna ofiara ,która przed moimi oczami odnawia się bez końca,ciągle,wszędzie i dla wszystkich wielki dramat Kalwarii!

Na nieszczęście kiedy się zastanawiam nad tym nie umiem zanurzyć się w wierze,która pozwala widzieć.Chciałem zrozumieć,szukać wyjaśnień,po- równań...Jak bardzo nie miałem racji!Tajemnica przekracza rozum,lecz jest słodka dla serca.Czy to nie jest całkowicie proste,że Miłość przekracza granice naszych słabych możliwości?Ty mnie kochasz oto całe wyjaśnienie tajemnicy.To mi z rozkoszą wystarczy.Przemieniasz Siebie,aby przyjąć moją formę i zbliżyć się do mnie.Ofiarowujesz się,

ponieważ błędy nas dzieliły a ofiara zmazuje je.

Pages from The Mass of a Soul.

The dove — Saint Scholastica's symbol, but also of consecrated virgins in general, here perched with her little ones among thorns. What did Sister Bernadette have in mind when she created this illustration? Perhaps she can teach souls the finding of Christ among thorns, nourished by His Most Precious Blood.

AFTERWORD
For Their Sake
I Consecrate Myself

A Monk of Silverstream Priory

PERHAPS A YEAR BEFORE RÓŻA WOLSKA WAS
born in 1927, the Swiss priest and theologian Maurice Zundel wrote
the following lines:

> It is more important to make men *see* the Church in the
> divine purity of her inner life than to praise or defend her.
> She is the Mother whose catholic heart embraces the souls
> even of those who know her not, even of those who would
> destroy her.[1]

These words are, I believe, profoundly pertinent to the life of
Róża Wolska, later known as Sister Bernadette of the Cross. Every
baptized soul participates in the reality which is the Church, becoming not only a member but also in some sense an image of her. Yet
Sister Bernadette's life is all the more an incarnation of the Church's
mystery — if one may speak that way — because her state of life as a
consecrated virgin conforms her all the more to the Church's bridal
and maternal character.

In her reparative death, we also glimpse something of Sister
Bernadette's participation in the mystery of Christ's suffering. Her
"unwearied prayer rises every hour in praise or in supplication towards
the most pure Beauty which alone can fill our souls, starved upon lit-
tleness, with its glory."[2] Sister Bernadette becomes a window through
which something of the glory of this Beauty reaches us. And that is

---

1 Maurice Zundel, *The Splendour of the Liturgy* (London: Sheed and Ward,
1939), Preface, p. ix (original emphasis). The first version of this work was
published in 1926.
2 Ibid.

what this book is about. Its purpose is "to make men see the light which illumines her countenance and the dream of Beauty glowing in it, and seeing them, recognise her as the dwelling-place of the Spirit and the Bride of the Lord."[3]

Sister Bernadette was an enthusiastic artist. She also appreciated music and enjoyed a certain facility in making it. But she did not let that get in the way of following a higher Art and a higher Song with her whole life: that of conformity to Christ, the True Image of the Father, Who is the Song of the Father. Although she might not have said it like this, Sister Bernadette recognized that the problem with every canvas is that it has edges and the problem with every piece of music is that it ends. These problems do not stop with art, however. They permeate life. The problem with every golden leaf in fall is that it won't be there next spring. The problem with every laugh is that it stops.

And yet, who would want a never-ending piece of canvas, or a piece of music which never cadenced? Or an everlasting laugh? They are good as you pass through them, but the moment they gain self-consciousness and are prolonged artificially, they wither. This brings us to another problem: the finite beauty we create and experience often seems wasted.

Why does God waste beauty? If you walk through the forest on a fall day, and the leaves are falling and carpeting the ground with gold and orange (as they do in our monastery's forest), how can one not wonder why it is that God is letting all this beauty go to waste? Is He careless? Is it just that this earth is not all that beautiful but seems so to us? These do not seem to be satisfying answers. Is it because God is so rich with beauty that He can create a certain sort of beauty which in the act of wasting itself is all the more beautiful? Or is it a case of the artist who doesn't mind the colors running together on His palette as He mixes them for His painting?

I know how, sometimes, as one mixes the watercolors on a china dish, they seem almost too beautiful on the palette to waste on the uncertainty of the paper. How many people are there who mistake the palette for the painting in their lives and resist the hand of God which would blend and temper them to create His own masterpiece?

---

3   Ibid.

I am unable to present a tidy answer for these questions. Instead, I am going to raise the stakes and turn from painters' palettes and falling leaves to human beings. Why in the world does God let people die? In fact, why does He treat His saints so badly sometimes? For if the problem with every canvas is that it has an edge, the problem or tragedy with Sister Bernadette is that her life ended.

The error of the abstract artists was to mistake the palette for the finished painting. And yet, when one turns from an artist's palette and sees the beautiful painting he has created, the splattered palette is forgotten. Only someone who has never seen or properly appreciated a finished painting could mistake the messy palette for a final product. And perhaps that is what happened to the abstract artists. They had never really *seen* a complete painting — they could not value order in art because they could not see order in the universe.

And so I would like to share some reflections occasioned by reading this life of Sister Bernadette. I discovered Sister Bernadette's life and meditated on it in the weeks surrounding the feast of All Saints and the commemoration of All Souls, 2021. Her presence profoundly illuminated those and other feasts. Her life is a challenging example of brilliant colors which seem suddenly to become muddied in the creation of a painting hidden from us. She is like an autumn leaf, glowing in the sunshine, which flutters on to the road. A car passes, and it is no more.

However, if we can't solve the tragedy of leaves falling in the autumn, we may not be able to solve the dilemma of God's beloved children rotting away either. I do not propose definitive answers, as I said before. But when we stop and take a seat with Sister Bernadette in the cloister garden, we can learn a lot from her about the hope which we cherish of heaven, and how we can know, love, and serve God in this life so as to be happy with Him in the next.

The saints make us ask: Is life a cosmic blasphemy?

It seems that any real contact with the saints will inevitably bring us, usually sooner rather than later, into contact with two things: beauty and suffering. Both have a quality of transcendence — that is, they participate in supernatural realities — and yet, of necessity, they

are also very "this worldly", and are filled with the poignant specifics
of any event which takes place in the limits of space and time.

Suffering and beauty: they are intensely present in the lives of
saints because in the current dispensation or economy of salva-
tion—management, if you will—we live in a fallen world which
was redeemed by the death of the Son of the All-Good God. In
this fact of facts, beauty and suffering are both present in the same
mystery of God's relation to our world. Beauty: because anything
that has something of God in it will of necessity participate in
the Truth, Goodness, and Beauty of God. Suffering: because there
are still sufferings which are "lacking" to the Body of Christ and
must be "filled up" by the Church. God willed to make suffering
redemptive—necessary even—not because God willed suffering,
but because, in the redemption of the world through the suffering
of His Son, He chose not to abolish (as yet) this effect of the
fall but to provide the key for its transformation and ordering
towards the Good.

Even so, the "problem of suffering" remains, and it is brought
all the more sharply into focus in the lives of saints who seem the
least deserving of evil, and whose goodness provides all the more
brilliant a backdrop against which the ravages of sickness and
death are highlighted to the extreme. It brings us, also, to face an
earth-shattering dilemma, one in which we find ourselves either
thrown back on the hope of a future re-creation of all things or
else forced to conclude that life, in all its aspects, is the most stu-
pendous farce, one which should be obliterated as soon as possible.

I say this because in the lives of such people as Saint Thérèse
of Lisieux (1873–1897) and Saint Elizabeth of the Trinity (1880–
1906), to name some better-known examples besides that of Sister
Bernadette, we see youth and beauty, talent and strength, alive to
God, to nature, and to their fellow men; they are full of laughter
and thought, sensitive to beauty as much as to suffering—we
see these people annihilated, disfigured, emaciated, disappearing
from view until death takes them and they are...no more. If
there is not something (banal as it sounds) "bigger and better,"
a reality of which they are still part, then the very existence of
their momentary lives becomes a screaming blasphemy of reality,

a blasphemy which dangles life in the void of non-existence for a cosmic second before obliterating it.

I say "blasphemy" because, to my mind, there is nothing more terrible than the thought that beauty and life can exist only to cease: existing at one time, they will not be at another. For something good to exist which does not endure in some fashion — can there be anything more horrible? As waste and lack of purpose are contrary to the qualities of proportion and meaning that true Beauty and Goodness possess, finitude imposes a waste and purposelessness which corrupts such qualities.

So it is that the saints challenge us, not only because we see in them the highest human qualities made still more beautiful by grace, but because we see them reduced to non-existence in a process which we call living and dying but which they call the threshold of eternal life.

It happened that I was directing the schola for All Saints and All Souls this year. We also had a Solemn Profession at our monastery on the feast of All Saints. Several of Fra Angelico's paintings adorned the booklet for the ceremony. Against the backdrop of the feast and profession ceremonies, I found truths striking me in a new way once I could contemplate them "incarnate" in Róża Wolska.

A fundamental impression was the "cloud of witnesses" which we were approaching. *Vidi turbam magnam* is the first antiphon of the feast. In a few strokes of melody we can almost take our places among the dance of Fra Angelico's saints as they enter Jerusalem the Golden. It cannot be abstract. It must be concrete: I know *this* saint, I know *that* one, and, "Oh, I'm *so happy* to see you!"

We are citizens of the Jerusalem which is above, Saint Paul says (Eph 2:19). As citizens of the Heavenly Jerusalem, however, we are strangers and sojourners on this earth. We are travellers, as Saint Columbanus points out, and must not mistake the road of this life for the destination which is heaven.[4] Perhaps this world is like a palette, and, sad as it can seem, the colors are sometimes destroyed because they are meant for the new creation which will go beyond all our hopes and dreams.

---

4   Cf. Saint Columbanus, Sermon VII.

To forget death is to be robbed of hope

Some have found Saint Benedict's dictum "to keep death daily before one's eyes"[5] to be morbid. I ask them: is it morbid to keep happiness, and the meaning and worth of our actions, daily before our eyes? For if death is not the gateway to eternal joy with God, then our lives have no meaning and we should have no happiness. In fact, if death could not be kept daily before our eyes as the hope of a reality that has the potential to make everything in our life beautiful and enduring, then having a daily existence at all would not be worthwhile.

Is not the Crucifix hung on a wall to "keep death daily before our eyes?" Is not the Holy Sacrifice of the Mass to keep death daily before our eyes? "Admit us, we beseech Thee into the company of the Saints . . . Wherefore, calling to mind the blessed Passion, Resurrection, and glorious Ascension . . ."[6] we pray in the Canon of the Mass. Is not every Communion to show the death of the Lord until He comes (cf. 1 Cor 11:26)? And the Rosary — "now and at the hour of our death" is a prayer worth praying only if both life and death are meaningful, and if both influence each other.

Yet the sufferings of Christ are also present in the "death of his holy ones" (Ps 115:15). For all of us who daily pass by a Crucifix, receive the Host, and pray our beads without keeping in mind the hope, joy, and meaning they should bring us, the saints are able to wake us up, shock us, and remind us that to be Christian is also to be cruciform.

From time to time the traditional Requiem Liturgy is criticized as a dreary and sin-obsessed ritual, incongruous in light of the hope which Christians should cherish in the mercy of God and the joy of the Resurrection. I would disagree. If the Requiem is somber it is because it is in touch with the reality of man's frailty and mortality. Indeed, those aspects of man would drive us to despair were they considered in themselves. Peace and joy in the hope of the resurrection that will be ours acquire reality only when they are honestly brought into relation with our mortality. To divorce the two and pretend there is only light is not to give the hope of life

---

5   *Rule*, ch. 4.

6   Cf. prayers of the Roman Canon *Nobis quoque peccatoribus* and *Unde et memores*.

its true place; rather, it is to contracept that hope by estranging it from the neediness which is the soil in which the supernatural fruit of hope can grow.

Similarly, white vestments and joyful Mass formularies are sometimes proposed as more appropriate in funerals for Christians whose holiness and virtue is easily recognised. In meditating on the death of Sister Bernadette, however, I found this proposition to be powerfully belied by the joy which shone through the Requiem texts as I pondered and sang them in the light of Sister Bernadette's life.

The antiphon sung at the graveside particularly struck me. In *In paradisum*...[7] the melody surges (there is no other word for it) up: "May the Angels lead thee into paradise." For Sister Bernadette it is dawn, her dawn. She wondered what it would be like to meet Melchizedek in heaven. Now the throngs of prophets, patriarchs, and martyrs are coming to her. Another star from the sky which Abraham beheld as God promised him an innumerable posterity has found its place in the firmament. *In tuo adventu suscipiant te Martyres*...yes, those thirty-odd sisters of hers who had died in the Warsaw Uprising twenty years earlier when Róża Wolska was just a teenager. *Et perducat te in civitatem sanctam Jerusalem*. It is your Holy City now, Rozmarynka. You are a *filia Sion*, a daughter of Sion now. "Go forth and see how she has been crowned."[8] What? you say. I cannot see. No. But you will. When it is *our* Holy City, you will see.

If the Requiem Mass is at all a "dark" Mass, it is because it is a dawn Mass, and there is only a glimmer of the light which the darkness does not comprehend. It is a dawn Mass, but it is her dawn, not ours. For us to say *Lux perpetua luceat ei* is to acknowledge that we do not yet know *that* light on earth. No, it is her dawn, her dawn Mass: it is for *her* to say *Lux fulgebit hodie super nos*...[9]

Et cum Lazaro, quondam paupere...the descending triad which follows the elongated podatus on *Lazaro* leaves an utterly wistful taste

---

7   "May the Angels lead thee into paradise: may the Martyrs receive thee at thy coming, and lead thee into the holy city of Jerusalem. May the choir of Angels receive thee, and mayest thou have eternal rest with Lazarus, who once was poor."

8   Cf. Office of Saint Gertrude.

9   Cf. the Introit of Dawn Mass of Christmas, "A light shall shine upon us this day."

in the singer's mouth. Lazarus, once a poor man—you were like him, Sister, you were covered with sores also. Now you rejoice together; you are no longer feeding from the crumbs of the Master's table.

And there is a responsory: *Subvenite, Sancti Dei.*[10] Jump up and run with a laugh, scattering the golden light of beatitude, O you angels of God! *Occurite:* receive her, offer her as she always wished to be offered, *in conspectu Altissimi.* Like every monk and nun she suffered because the union was not complete in this life. Death was lacking. Now it is the full return to the Father.[11]

Suscipiat te Christus, qui vocavit te . . . You sang your *Suscipe*; it was Christ Who called you. You remembered that you had an inexplicable urge to enter the monastery and only later did you begin to understand what that call really meant. *Media autem nocte.*[12] Yes, in the midst of that abysmal suffering when the life drained out of a thirty-five year old woman—*clamor factus est*—what dispositions filled her weakness as she received Communion for the last time? She was probably not thinking lofty and pious thoughts. In weakness, pain, and exhaustion, her being was oriented towards God because when she had possessed all her faculties, she had persevered in facing Him, dedicating her all to Him. And now? *Ecce, sponsus venit.* He. *Exite obviam Christo Domino.* And her joy was full.

What was the color for?

When I compared the life of Sister Bernadette to an artist's palette I omitted one important consideration. I said we couldn't see the painting for which she was ruthlessly spent. We might not be able to see it fully, but perhaps we already know what she was spent

10   "Come to her assistance, ye Saints of God, come forth to meet her, ye Angels of the Lord, receiving her soul, offering it in the sight of the Most High. May Christ receive thee Who has called thee, and may the Angels lead thee into Abraham's bosom." Responsory sung in religious communities when news of a death in the Order is received, and at a funeral for the reception of the body.
11   Cf. Mother Geneviève Gallois, *The Life of Little Saint Placid* (Homer Glen, NY: St. Augustine Academy Press, 2017), 102.
12   "The five wise virgins took oil in their vessels with the lamps: and at midnight there was a cry made: Behold the Bridegroom cometh: go ye forth to meet Christ the Lord"—Communion Antiphon, *Quinque prudentes virgines,* from the Mass of a Virgin not a Martyr, *Dilexisti.* This is the source for the remainder of the quotes in this paragraph.

for, what she was wasted for: the Church and Priests. Perhaps the order of things was reversed: here a bride lays down her life for the unfaithful bridegrooms. Those other Christs, who should have cherished the Church as their own flesh (cf. Eph 5), who should have loved to the death. Their infidelity, instead of repulsing this bride, caused her to take their place and offer her own life instead. "Cut me into strips," she said, "only let them return to You." The Communion Antiphon of the Votive Mass of the Most Blessed Sacrament brings this home in a most poignant way: "Therefore whosoever shall eat this Bread, or drink the Chalice of the Lord unworthily, shall be guilty of the Body and of the Blood of the Lord" (1 Cor 11:27). If anyone wants to know what an unworthy Communion *does*, what it *looks* like, let him look at Sister Bernadette, who took its effects upon herself in reparation.

We can go further. Her life and self-offering were a *Canon Missae*, a life lived according to the "rule of offering." That is what *canon* means in Greek: the rule or law of the Mass's sacrifice. Zundel observes, "The Mass is a mystery, which must be made our living experience. And that experience is no less than a death for love."[13] As a "death for love," Sister Bernadette's life can, I believe, truly give us insight into the Mass:

> Wherefore, O most merciful Father, we humbly pray and beseech Thee... that Thou wouldst vouchsafe to receive and bless this gift, this holy and unspotted sacrifice... which in the first place we offer Thee for Thy holy Catholic Church.[14]

Here is the culminating incarnation of the reality of a life lived in union with the Mass, a life born aloft in a profession *Suscipe* which found its ultimate fruitfulness in another: *Suscipe, Sancte Pater ... hanc immaculatam hostia*m... receive this pure offering.[15]

If the mystery of "cruciformity" is central to the Christian life, we should not balk at reading the liturgical offices which treat of Our Lord's passion as applicable (all proportion guarded) to ourselves. Let us turn to the texts of Passiontide and let them illumine the life of Sister Bernadette for us.

---

13 Zundel, *Splendour of the Liturgy*, Preface to the second edition, xi.
14 Cf. the *Te Igitur* of the Roman Canon.
15 Cf. Offertory prayer *Suscipe, sancte Pater*.

Plorans ploravit in nocte, et lacrimae in maxillis ejus, "Weeping she hath wept in the night, and her tears are on her cheeks" (Lam 1:2). Was not Sister Bernadette's cry of offering but a transposition of that cry which concludes the Lamentations of the office of Tenebrae? *Jerusalem, Jerusalem, convertere ad Dominum Deum tuum* . . . Jerusalem, Jerusalem, return to the Lord your God.

Vos fugam capietis, et ego vadam immolari pro vobis . . . you shall flee, while I go to be immolated for you.[16] She was "offered because she herself willed it."[17] And then that glimmer in the third chapter of Lamentations:

> The mercies of the Lord that we are not consumed: because his commiserations have not failed. They are new every morning, great is thy faithfulness. The Lord is my portion, said my soul: therefore will I wait for him. The Lord is good to them that hope in him, to the soul that seeketh him. It is good to wait with silence for the salvation of God. It is good for a man, when he hath borne the yoke from his youth. He shall sit solitary, and hold his peace: because he hath taken it up upon himself. He shall put his mouth in the dust, if so be there may be hope. He shall give his cheek to him that striketh him, he shall be filled with reproaches. For the Lord will not cast off for ever (Lam 3:22–31).

Monastic profession: Becoming a lovescape crucified

We say that Christ "suffered for our sins." Do we actually know what we are saying? One day, singing in the schola for a Votive Mass of the Most Blessed Sacrament — familiar as that Mass is for our community — the chant of the Communion struck me in a new light: "For as often as you shall eat this Bread, and drink the Chalice, you shall shew the death of the Lord, until he come" (1 Cor 11:26). Is it to show, to announce the death, to make it present, yes in the Eucharistic elements, but also in ourselves by the ineffable union which takes place when we receive Christ. "Him I would learn to know . . . and what it means to share His sufferings, moulded into the pattern of His death" (Phil 3:10, Knox). Sister Bernadette is an example of

---

16   Second Responsory for Matins of Holy Thursday.
17   Cf. Fifth Antiphon at Lauds on Holy Thursday.

what it means to "show" the death of the Lord to the fullest extent. And yet it was all contained in seed-form in her monastic profession.

When that profession chart, on which she "signed her life away" was placed on the altar, under the corporal, all subsequent offerings were represented there, made present by anticipation, and united with the offering on the altar. "Wherefore in memory of the blessed Passion, Resurrection, and glorious Ascension . . . we offer thee this victim."[18]

United to Christ, we become co-responsible — in a sense — for the redemption of the whole universe. "Behold," Zundel remarks to the soul who has just received Communion, "the entire universe is in your hands like a host, to be consecrated by your charity, and restored to its Divine vocation, which is to love and to sing."[19]

To love and to sing: this seems to me but another way of expressing Saint Benedict's fundamental desire "to put nothing before the Work of God" and "to prefer nothing to the love of Christ."[20] For if prayer is but the expression of love, the sung Divine Office is for Saint Benedict the highest expression of prayer. And this prayer finds a Eucharistic summit in the Mass: "Faith teaches us what divine amplitude this music can attain when He who is the ineffable Song of the Father sings in silence beneath the veil of the Host."[21] A special insight into this Eucharistic quality of Benedictine life was given to Mother Mectilde who began the Institute of Benedictines of Perpetual Adoration. In her short work, *The True Spirit*, in which she explains the dispositions which should characterize the life of her nuns, Mother Mectilde returns again and again to the mystery of Christ-likeness. Approaching it from many angles, perhaps her most sustained exposition concerns the "states of the Host" — that is, aspects of Christ's life, death, and resurrection which are particularly highlighted by His presence in the Eucharist, and the ways in which each religious can be "conformed" to them. In her own quiet and joyful way Sister Bernadette eminently embodies several of the dispositions outlined by Mother Mectilde. Although they can seem strange and even harsh to modern readers, Mother

---

18   Cf. Prayer of the Roman Canon *Unde et memores*.
19   Zundel, *Splendour of the Liturgy*, 246.
20   Cf. *Rule*, ch. 43 and 72.
21   Zundel, 147.

Mectilde's insights are better understood in the light of a concrete living expression of them such as Sister Bernadette's.

Monastic profession cuts to the heart of this mystery of cruciformity and Christoformity. On the Solemnity of All Saints we also had, as I mentioned, a Solemn Profession. A particularly striking part of the rite is when the newly professed monk prostrates himself in the middle of the Oratory and is covered with a black funeral pall while the following chant is sung by the Schola: *Mortuus sum et vita mea abscondita est cum Christo in Deo*, "I am dead, and my life is hid with Christ in God" (cf. Col 3:3). And then there is a verse, a soaring cantilena of pneumatic dew, droplets of human tears illuminated by God's providential Charity, a shower of sparks in the night of this life, in the cold of evil, in the fear and uncertainty that must clutch every heart. A laugh, a smile, a joy echoing from a thousand thousand miles away, beside you, right there, close: *Non moriar, sed vivam.* "I shall not die, I shall live and praise the Lord" (Ps 117:17). That is what the saints do. That is what monastic profession is about. That is why Sister Bernadette can die and not have failed in attaining ultimate meaning and joy. And yet it is death, a death which is *pretiosa*, precious, as the second verse of the responsory reminds us.

In his poem *Wreck of the Deutschland*, Gerard Manley Hopkins speaks of this cruciform nature of the Christian life with reference to Saint Francis of Assisi:

> Joy fall to thee, father Francis,
> Drawn to the Life that died;
> With the gnarls of the nails in thee, niche of the lance, his
> Lovescape crucified . . .

It is the saints who, "drawn to the Life that died," are the ones who "would learn to know . . . what it means to share his sufferings," be "moulded into the pattern of His death, in the hope of achieving resurrection from the dead" (Phil 3:10–11, Knox). Thus it is that we should see that strange — oh, beautiful, yes, but also terrifying — transformation of a man or a woman into another "lovescape crucified." Already made integral to the Christian in baptism, monastic profession makes this transformation more explicit.

I hate practical takeaways

Perhaps we can be tempted to ask if there are "practical takeaways" from the life of Sister Bernadette. I dislike forcing that question; yet the difference here is that I do not think it is a forced question. And I also think there are truly *practical* and life-changing truths which, when we *see* them, are quite simply... life-changing! And that is because when we *see* them, we are that much closer to *living* them.

Saints are not people without problems. But they are people who carry on anyway, knowing that "not what thou art, nor what thou hast been, beholdeth God with His merciful eyes, but what thou wouldst be."[22] Extraordinary experiences and sufferings are by no means necessary for becoming a true lovescape crucified. Entirely ordinary virtues and spiritual fruits are sufficient; and these are nothing else but perseverance in prayer, a fundamental openness to and trust in God's providence, and a this-minute readiness to give ourselves completely to the obligations of our state in life. The fruits which accompany such living are joy, hope, trust, and peace.

The only difficult thing about these ordinary ways is that, being so ordinary, we don't (or won't) often see how they have become *Divine* means ever since the Incarnation and our incorporation into its mystery in Baptism. As adopted sons in the Son, there is nothing left for us to do but sing, *Suscipe me, Sancte Pater, omnipotens aeterne Deus,* and rejoice when that Father from Whom all fatherhood in heaven and on earth takes its name bends down and begins to form us into lovescapes crucified — yes, and to rejoice even when it seems like He is muddying the colors of our life.

---

22   Rummer Godden, *In This House of Brede* (Providence, RI: Cluny Media, 2020), 57, quoting ch. 57 of *The Cloud of Unknowing.*

APPENDIX

Monasteries of the Institute of Benedictine Nuns of Perpetual Adoration of the Blessed Sacrament in Poland (Moniales Ordinis Sancti Benedicti Adorationis Perpetuae Sanctissimi Sacramenti)

General website of the Polish Federation of the Benedictine Nuns of the Blessed Sacrament:
www.benedyktynki.info

Rynek Nowego Miasta 2
00–229 WARSZAWA
Phone: (22) 831 49 62
e-mail: mniszki@osbap.org
www.benedyktynki-sakramentki.org (Polish/English)

ul. Przedwiośnie 76/78
51–211 WROCŁAW
Phone: (71) 330 41 04
e-mail: sakramentki@wroclaw.opoka.org.pl
www.benedyktynki-sakramentki.wroclaw.com

ul. Rawicza 32
08–110 SIEDLCE
Phone: (25) 632 27 34
e-mail: benedyktynki.sakramentki@o2.pl
www.benedyktynki-sakramentki-siedlce.com

FURTHER INFORMATION

Monasteries with English Websites

Benedictine Monks of Perpetual Adoration
Silverstream Priory
Stamullen, County Meath, Ireland
www.cenacleosb.org

Benedictine Nuns of Perpetual Adoration
Priorij Nazareth, Klooster Oude Munt
Van Wevelickhovenstraat 1
NL-5931 KS Tegelen, The Netherlands
www.oudemunt.nl (Dutch/English)

About Mother Mectilde

The Mystery of Incomprehensible Love. Brooklyn, NY: Angelico Press, 2020.
   Includes a selection of Mother's writings, a biography by Canon G. A.
   Simon, and an essay by Dom Jean Leclercq, OSB.
*The "Breviary of Fire": Letters by Mother Mectilde of the Blessed Sacrament,
   Chosen and Arranged by the Countess of Châteauvieux*. Brooklyn, NY:
   Angelico Press, 2021. A collection of letters on various themes of the
   spiritual life, with historical and interpretive essays by Fr. Paul Milcent,
   CJM, Fr. Michel Dupuy, PSS, and Msgr. Charles Molette.
www.mechtylda.info: website about Mother Mectilde (in Polish).
www.mectilde.info: website with photocopies of original manuscripts and
   publications by Mother Mectilde, her biography, religious books from
   the seventeenth century that inspired her, and an alphabetical catalog
   of all her writings (in French).

ABOUT THE AUTHOR

JADWIGA STABIŃSKA (1935–2016) was born in Grodno (then in Poland, today in Belarus). In May of 1951 she passed her *matura* exam (high school exit exam) at the High School in Ełk, and in October of that same year she started studying psychology at the University of Warsaw. On December 7, 1954 she entered the cloister of the Benedictine Nuns of Perpetual Adoration in Warsaw. Her vestition took place on July 2, 1955. She made her first profession of vows on October 26, 1957, and took her solemn vows on October 30, 1960. In the 1960s, she began her work as a writer. Many of her articles, poems, and translations were published in various Catholic magazines. She also published numerous books which captured her interests and reflections, including *Królowa Jadwiga* (*Queen Hedwig*, 1969); *Mistrz Wincenty* (*Master Vincent*, 1973); *Siostra Faustyna Kowalska: duchowość i doktryna* (*Sister Faustina Kowalska: Spirituality and Doctrine*, 1976); *Danina krwi: z wojennych dziejów klasztoru sióstr sakramentek w Warszawie* (*Blood Offering: Wartime History of the Monastery of Benedictine Nuns of Perpetual Adoration of the Blessed Sacrament in Warsaw*, 1977). She also translated various writings of Mother Mectilde of the Blessed Sacrament and the final poems of Saint Elizabeth of the Trinity. Her most important work was the book *Oblicza kontemplacji* (*Faces of Contemplation*, 1977) for which the Holy Father John Paul II himself thanked her. She received numerous awards and recognitions for her work. On January 29, 1990, her autobiographical novel *Blanka: opowieść prawdziwa* (*Blanka: A True Story*) received an award for youth literature in a literary competition organized by Wydawnictwo Księgarni św. Wojciecha (Saint Adalbert Bookstore Publishing House) in Poznań. She died on January 22, 2016, after a long battle with cancer at 81 years of age, 59 of which were spent in monastic profession.

ABOUT THE TRANSLATOR

JUSTYNA KRUKOWSKA holds an MA in American Literature from the University of Białystok in Poland and a Master of Theological Studies from the International Theological Institute in Austria. A native of Poland, she has worked for various Catholic institutions in California, where she resides with her husband and children.

CPSIA information can be obtained
at www.ICGtesting.com
Printed in the USA
JSHW010913020622
26588JS00012B/330